STUDENT UNIT

A2 Law
UNIT 4
AQA

Module 4: Criminal Law

Ian Yule

A2 Law

Philip Allan Updates
Market Place
Deddington
Oxfordshire
OX15 0SE

Tel: 01869 338652
Fax: 01869 337590
e-mail: sales@philipallan.co.uk
www.philipallan.co.uk

© Philip Allan Updates 2004

ISBN 1 84489 000 7

All rights reserved; no part of this publication may be reproduced, stored in a retrieval system, or transmitted, in any form or by any means, electronic, mechanical, photocopying, recording or otherwise without either the prior written permission of Philip Allan Updates or a licence permitting restricted copying in the United Kingdom issued by the Copyright Licensing Agency Ltd, 90 Tottenham Court Road, London W1P 9HE.

This guide has been written specifically to support students preparing for the AQA A2 Law Unit 4 examination. The content has been neither approved nor endorsed by AQA and remains the sole responsibility of the author.

Printed by Information Press, Eynsham, Oxford

Environmental information
The paper on which this title is printed is sourced from managed, sustainable forests.

AQA Unit 4

Contents

Introduction
About this guide 4
How to use this guide 4
Learning strategies 4
Revision planning 5
Assessment objectives 5
Examination technique 5
Summary of main legal terms used in this guide 7

■ ■ ■

Content Guidance
About this section 10
Non-fatal offences 11
Murder 16
Voluntary manslaughter 20
Involuntary manslaughter 26
General defences 31
Critical evaluation of fatal and non-fatal offences 41

■ ■ ■

Questions and Answers
About this section 54
Q1 Non-fatal offences (I) 55
Q2 Non-fatal offences (II) 57
Q3 Grievous bodily harm and involuntary manslaughter 59
Q4 Unlawful and dangerous act manslaughter 68
Q5 Murder, provocation and intoxication 71
Q6 Murder, diminished responsibility and insanity 74
Q7 Malice aforethought 76

A2 Law

Introduction

About this guide
The AQA specification for the AS and A2 Law examinations is divided into six modules. Unit 4 is about **Criminal Law** and covers both non-fatal and fatal offences against the person. It is a substantive, i.e. 'real law', module, so it is important that you are able to use case law effectively.

The examination for this module is 1 hour 15 minutes. It comprises two questions from which you must select one. Each question consists of three parts. The first two parts, based on a scenario, deal with a non-fatal and a fatal offence. The third part is evaluative, and asks you to analyse either non-fatal or fatal offences, to consider possible criticisms and perhaps to suggest how the law could be reformed. This guide includes advice on approaching this part of the unit exam.

There are three sections to this guide:
- **Introduction** — this provides advice on how the guide should be used, an explanation of the skills and terminology required to complete the unit successfully and guidance on revision and examination techniques.
- **Content Guidance** — this sets out the specification content for Unit 4. It also contains references to cases which you will need to study for a sound understanding of each topic.
- **Questions and Answers** — this section provides seven questions which are followed by student answers. Examiner comments show why marks are awarded or withheld. The A-grade answers demonstrate how to employ case and statutory references to best effect.

How to use this guide
The Content Guidance section covers all the elements of the Unit 4 specification, breaking it down into manageable sections for study and learning. It is not intended to be a comprehensive and detailed set of notes for the unit — the material needs to be supplemented by further reading from textbooks and case studies.

When you have finished reading each section, make a summary of the factual material under the appropriate headings, incorporating additional material from your wider reading and research, and then test yourself by using the sample question(s) on that particular topic. By practising questions and assessing your answers against the examiner's comments you will learn how to use your knowledge and understanding effectively to improve your exam grade.

Learning strategies
It is essential to build up a good set of notes for successful A2 study. These notes need to be laid out clearly under the headings used in the Content Guidance section.

Your notes should contain accurate definitions and explanations together with relevant case and statutory references, and should be drawn not only from this guide but also from your wider reading. It is also recommended that you compile summaries of the most important cases — this will make it much easier to remember these cases and to use them in examination answers.

Revision planning

At this level of study, it is essential that you understand the need to learn factual information thoroughly — this should be done as the module is being taught. Don't leave it to the revision stage, otherwise you will find that there is simply too much detailed information to absorb. Remember that skimming over some notes or reading this guide is *not* revision if you have not already learnt the material.

The first stage of revision requires organisation of all your work. Ensure that:
- your class notes are up to date
- you have used the material in this guide effectively
- you have made accurate notes on any wider reading, especially of case studies

You should then summarise all of the material, organising it under the headings and sub-headings of the Unit 4 specification. During the revision period, you should go over all your notes and reduce them to manageable proportions. This is, in itself, an effective learning exercise. The act of summarising makes it easier to recall the material and should reduce the chance of forgetting parts of it in the examination. The greatest number of exam marks are not lost through failure to understand the material, but simply through forgetting fuller explanations and, in this unit particularly, how to use relevant cases.

Assessment objectives

Assessment objectives (AOs) are common to AS and A2 units and are intended to assess candidates' ability to:
- recall, select, deploy and develop knowledge and understanding of legal principles accurately and by means of examples
- analyse legal material, issues and situations, and evaluate and apply the appropriate legal rules and principles
- present a logical and coherent argument and communicate relevant material in a clear and effective manner, using correct legal terminology

Examination technique

Case references
The importance of case references cannot be overemphasised. A 'case-free' answer rarely obtains more than a D or E grade, and will more often be awarded a U grade. Without appropriate case references, it is simply not possible to demonstrate a sound understanding of relevant law. Remember, the cases you have been taught do not just

'illustrate' that rule of law; in many cases they *are* the law. Be aware that the mark scheme often prevents examiners from awarding marks if there is no reference to case or statutory authorities, so omitting these references can seriously lower your grade.

Matching cases to the correct legal rule

Many candidates appear to believe that as long as some cases are mentioned, it does not matter too much if they are the right ones. Look carefully at the A- and C-grade answers to questions 3 and 7 in the Question and Answer section, and you will recognise the importance of using cases correctly. When revising, make a point of learning the correct case for each offence in terms of *actus reus* and *mens rea*.

Using cases

It is rarely necessary or desirable to describe at length the facts of the cases cited — the important part of a case is the legal rule it created or demonstrates. For example, if discussing *R v Nedrick*, the candidate should explain the legal rule regarding oblique intent that the case established — that the members of the jury can return a guilty verdict in a murder trial if they believe that the defendant foresaw death or serious injury as virtually certain — rather than reciting the full facts of the case. Although it is a good idea to make a brief reference to the facts, the only occasion when a more detailed description would be required is if a question scenario matches the facts of a case very closely.

Omissions

This is the greatest single source of lost marks. Spend time reading the question and deciding which legal topics are relevant to the scenario — both offences and defences. Draft summaries for each offence and defence, like that on page 15, and remember to include references to important cases. In comparing the A- and C-grade answers to questions 3 and 7 in the Question and Answer section, note the material which is omitted from the C-grade answers and the inadequate explanations they give.

QWC marks

There are 10 marks for each A2 paper for quality of written communication. The easiest way to lose some of these is to misspell basic legal words such as *grievous, defendant, deterrence, assault, sentence*. Finally, check your spelling, use paragraphs correctly and make your handwriting as clear as possible.

Planning your answers effectively

When you look at the A-grade answers you will recognise that they have a clear structure, usually demonstrated straight away by a simple, accurate and relevant first sentence. C-grade answers lack this element of planning and structure. You should read the exam question carefully and make sure you understand what it is asking, and then make a short plan — it could be in the form of a spider diagram or just a series of headings and subheadings. After this, read the question again to check that your plan is both relevant and accurate. Don't worry about crafting a lengthy introduction to your answers — this is not an English exam. Look carefully at how the A-grade answers start and model your own technique on these.

Time planning
Contrary to popular belief, few students have a problem with lack of time in the examination. By doing homework essays and timed or practice examination essays you will learn whether you are a quick or a slow writer. If you feel that you are likely to have a time problem, planning your response is even more vital. There is no point in wasting time on material which is either inaccurate or irrelevant.

Those who finish early — and this will apply to most candidates — should first check their answers to ensure that they have included key legal rules and appropriate cases. Next they should look at their plans to ensure that they have covered all the points. If at the end of this process there is still time left, they should consider what additional material can quickly be added, such as a further case or, in an s.20 malicious wounding or grievous bodily harm answer, a short reference to s.18, some extra details on a type of defence, and so on. In the majority of exam scripts, it would be possible to improve the overall result by almost one grade (which can be as little as 1 or 2 marks) by adding such material.

Summary of main legal terms used in this guide

Actus reus
Actus reus is the physical element required for criminal liability which can comprise an act, an omission or a state of affairs. It has to be the voluntary, controlled act of the defendant. Key terms for the concept of *actus reus* are outlined below:

omission: the failure to act in circumstances where the law imposes a duty to do so. Examples include where the defendant has created a dangerous situation (*R v Miller*), where the defendant has assumed a responsibility (*R v Stone and Dobinson*), or where the defendant's contract of employment requires him or her to act in the interests of the safety of others (*R v Pitwood*).

causation: the legal rule which requires the prosecution to prove that the defendant was 'the cause' of the prohibited consequence. Two rules are the factual 'but for' rule (*R v White*), and the legal rule that the defendant must have made 'a significant contribution' to the unlawful outcome (*R v Cheshire*).

Mens rea
Mens rea is the mental element of criminal liability which can be intention, recklessness or gross negligence. Key terms for the concept of *mens rea* are outlined below:

intention: can be **direct**, where it is the defendant's aim, purpose or objective to achieve the unlawful result, or **oblique**, where defendants can argue that although they caused the unlawful outcome, they did so in circumstances where that was not their intention. This requires the jury to consider the elements of probability and foreseeability. The leading cases are those of *R v Nedrick* and *R v Woollin*, which created the rule of 'foresight of virtually certain consequences'.

recklessness: for all non-fatal offences, this is 'Cunningham' or 'subjective' recklessness — the conscious taking of an unjustified risk. This means the prosecution must prove that the defendant recognised the risk which was being taken.

gross negligence: only applies to manslaughter; the leading case is *R* v *Adomato*. It is based on the tort of negligence with the additional requirement that the defendant 'showed such disregard for the life and safety of others as to amount to a crime against the state and conduct deserving punishment'.

transferred malice: the rule that if A intends to shoot and kill B but misses and kills C, the 'intention' aimed at B is transferred to C, and A is therefore guilty of C's murder.

coincidence of *actus reus* and *mens rea*: this rule requires these elements to occur together. Note the 'continuing act' or 'linked transactions' rule from the cases of *R* v *Thabo Meli* and *Fagan* v *Metropolitan Police Commissioner*.

Offences

murder: defined as 'unlawful killing with malice aforethought'. It is a specific intent crime requiring the prosecution to prove that the defendant intended either to kill or to inflict grievous bodily harm.

voluntary manslaughter: if the defendant pleads successfully either provocation or diminished responsibility to a murder charge, the jury may find him or her guilty of the lesser crime of voluntary manslaughter. This allows the judge to reflect the lower degree of criminal liability, usually by imposing a much lower sentence.

involuntary manslaughter: defined as 'unlawful killing without malice aforethought'. There are two types: gross negligence manslaughter (see above) and unlawful and dangerous act manslaughter. Unlawful and dangerous act manslaughter requires an act which is a crime, objectively dangerous and the cause of the victim's death. The *mens rea* of that crime becomes the *mens rea* for manslaughter.

Defences

provocation: requires evidence of provocation that caused the defendant to lose self-control in circumstances where a reasonable person would also have lost self-control and killed.

diminished responsibility: requires proof of an abnormality of mind (provided by psychiatric evidence) which caused a 'substantial impairment' in the defendant's mental responsibility for the killing.

consent: this defence is generally limited to minor non-fatal offences; for more serious non-fatal offences it only applies to activities such as organised sport, rough horse-play or surgery (including tattooing).

insanity: derives from the M'Naghten case and requires proof that the defendant was suffering from a defect of reason arising from disease of the mind, which caused him or her to be unable to appreciate the nature and quality of his or her actions, or that they were wrong in a criminal sense.

self-defence: both a common law and statutory defence. The main requirement is that the defendant used reasonable force. Excessive force will invalidate this defence (see *R* v *Martin*).

intoxication: this very limited defence is only effective in crimes of specific intent (murder and s.18 grievous bodily harm), where if the defendant is so drunk as to be unable to form the necessary mens rea, he or she will be convicted of the lesser offence of manslaughter or s.20 grievous bodily harm.

Content Guidance

The specification for Unit 4 outlined in this section is as follows:

Non-fatal offences
- Assault
- Battery
- S.47 assault occasioning actual bodily harm
- S.20 malicious wounding or inflicting grievous bodily harm
- S.18 wounding or causing grievous bodily harm with intent (to cause GBH)
- Summary of non-fatal offences
- Joint Charging Standard

Murder
- *Actus reus*: causation
- *Mens rea*: malice aforethought — specific intent

Voluntary manslaughter
- Diminished responsibility
- Provocation
- Suicide pact

Involuntary manslaughter
- Unlawful and dangerous act manslaughter
- Gross negligence manslaughter

Defences
- Insanity
- Automatism
- Consent
- Intoxication
- Self-defence/prevention of crime
- Mistake

Critical evaluation of fatal and non-fatal offences
Note that the current specification does not require the critical evaluation of defences.

Non-fatal offences

Unit 4 requires you to use the knowledge of non-fatal offences that you gained in Unit 3. The five different offences are:
- assault
- battery
- assault occasioning actual bodily harm (ABH)
- malicious wounding or inflicting grievous bodily harm (GBH)
- wounding or inflicting grievous bodily harm with intent (to cause GBH)

Assault and battery were two distinct crimes under common law and their separate existence is confirmed by s.39 of the **Criminal Justice Act 1988**. The other three more serious offences are defined in the **Offences Against the Person Act 1861**.

Assault

This is any act by which the defendant, intentionally or recklessly, causes the victim to apprehend immediate and unlawful personal violence. In other words, this offence can be described as 'a threat of violence which the victim believes to be a threat'. Accordingly, if any harm is caused, a more serious offence than assault has been committed, although the defendant may also have committed an assault, for example if the defendant has shouted at the victim 'I'm going to thump you' and then proceeds to do just that.

Actus reus of assault

In a typical case of an assault (as opposed to a battery), the defendant, by some physical movement, causes the victim to believe that he or she is about to be struck. There may even be an assault where the defendant has no intention to commit a battery but only to cause the victim to apprehend one. There is a tendency to enlarge the concept of assault by taking a generous view of 'immediacy', to include threats where the impending impact is more remote. In *Logdon* v *DPP* it was held that the defendant committed an assault by showing his victim a pistol in a drawer and declaring that he would hold her hostage.

In *Smith* v *Superintendent of Woking Police*, the defendant committed an assault by looking at the victim in her nightwear through a window, intending to frighten her. It was made clear in *R* v *Ireland* that an assault may be committed by words alone, or, as in that case, by silent telephone calls in which the caller 'intends by his silence to cause fear and he is so understood'.

There may also be an assault even where the defendant has no means of carrying out the threat. The issue to be decided in these cases is whether the defendant intends to cause the victim to believe that he or she can and will carry it out, and whether the victim believes this. It is clear that a threat to inflict harm at some future time cannot amount to an assault — an apprehension of immediate personal violence is essential. In *R* v *Constanza* it was held that there had been an assault when the victim read the letters which had been sent by a stalker and interpreted them as clear threats — there was a 'fear of violence at some time not excluding the immediate future'.

Battery

This is defined as: 'any act by which the defendant, intentionally or recklessly, inflicts unlawful personal violence'. Most batteries involve an assault, and the tendency is to refer generically to 'assaults'. Examples of battery include a push, a kiss or throwing a projectile or water which lands on another's body. Note that the battery need not be hostile or aggressive or rude. Many unwanted touchings are 'technical' batteries, and prosecutors are relied upon to avoid prosecutions of minor incidents. Since the merest touching without consent is a criminal offence, the demands of everyday life require that there be an implied consent to that degree of contact which is necessary or customary in ordinary life.

Actus reus of battery

This consists of the infliction of unlawful personal violence by the defendant. The term 'violence' here is misleading — all that is required for a battery is that the defendant touches the victim without consent or other lawful excuse. However, under the Joint Charging Standard, in practice a prosecution is most unlikely unless some injury has been caused. It is generally said that the defendant must have carried out an act, but there can be occasions where mere obstruction can be a battery. There may be a battery when the defendant inadvertently applies force to the victim and then wrongfully refuses to withdraw it. In *Fagan* v *Metropolitan Police Commissioner*, where the defendant accidentally drove his car on to a police officer's foot and then intentionally left it there, the court held that there was a continuing act, not a mere omission. It is also settled law that there can be a battery where there has been no direct contact with the victim's body — touching his or her clothing may be enough to constitute this offence, as in *R* v *Thomas*, where it was stated that touching the woman's skirt was equivalent to touching the woman herself.

Mens rea of assault and battery

The law is now settled that either intention or recklessness as to the respective elements is sufficient. After a brief period of uncertainty, it is now clear that common-law recklessness — 'the conscious taking of an unjustified risk' — not Caldwell recklessness, is the relevant test (see the cases of *R* v *Venna*, *R* v *Savage*, *R* v *Parmenter*). The defendant must actually foresee the risk of causing apprehension of violence, or the application, whichever the case may be.

Assault occasioning actual bodily harm (s.47)

Here the word 'assault' can mean either assault or battery, but most often it will refer to battery, the actual infliction of some unlawful violence rather than a threat of violence.

Actus reus

This offence is triable either way and carries a maximum sentence of 5 years' imprisonment — compare the maximum sentence of 6 months for common assault. The conduct element (*actus reus*) is an assault or battery which causes 'actual bodily harm'. This has been given the wide definition of 'any hurt or injury calculated to interfere with the health or comfort of the victim', provided it is not 'merely transient or trifling'. This was established in *R v Miller*.

One consequence of this definition is that it has been held to cover psychological harm — where the defendant causes the victim to become hysterical or to suffer substantial fear (see *R v Chan-Fook*). Note, however, that in *R v Morris* the Court of Appeal held that evidence from the victim's doctor that she suffered from anxiety, fear, tearfulness, sleeplessness and physical tension was insufficient to establish actual bodily harm.

Mens rea

The *mens rea* required for this offence is the same as for battery — intention or recklessness as to the application of some unlawful force to another. This important rule was established in the separate cases of *R v Savage* and *R v Parmenter*, where it was held by the House of Lords that the prosecution is not obliged for an s.47 offence to prove that the defendant intended to cause some actual bodily harm or was reckless as to whether such harm would be caused.

In *Savage*, the defendant admitted throwing the contents of her beer glass over the victim during a bar brawl. The glass slipped out of her hand and broke and a piece of glass cut the victim's wrist. The case established that a verdict of guilty may be returned upon proof of an assault together with proof of the fact that actual bodily harm was occasioned by the assault. This is a key legal point that examiners are looking for. Students must note that this is one of the most common mistakes made in examination answers. No marks are awarded for referring to the *mens rea* of s.47 actual bodily harm as intention or recklessness unless there is a clear reference to this issue and these cases.

R v Roberts confirms that the *mens rea* of s.47 actual bodily harm is the same as for assault or battery. In this case, the defendant gave a lift in his car to a girl. During the journey he made unwanted sexual advances, touching the girl's clothes. Frightened that he was going to rape her, she jumped out of the moving car, injuring herself. It was held that the defendant had committed the *actus reus* of s.47 by touching her clothes — sufficient for battery — and this act had caused her to suffer actual bodily harm. The defendant argued that he lacked the *mens rea* of the offence, because he had neither intended to cause her actual bodily harm, nor saw any risk of her suffering it as a result of his advances. This argument was rejected: the court held that the *mens rea* of battery was sufficient in itself, and there was no need for any extra *mens rea* regarding the actual bodily harm.

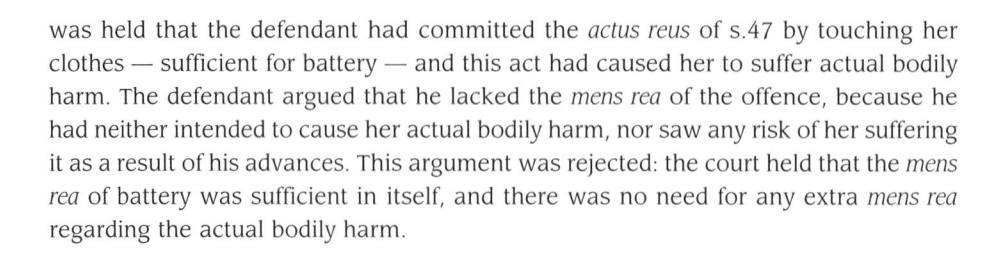

Malicious wounding or inflicting grievous bodily harm (s.20)

Actus reus

This section created the offence of unlawfully and maliciously wounding or inflicting grievous bodily harm. The conduct element here is the same as for the more serious offence under s.18 (see below). A wound is defined as an injury which breaks both the outer and inner skin; a bruise or a burst blood vessel in the eye would not amount to a wound — see *C (a minor)* v *Eisenhower*. In contrast, grievous bodily harm is defined as 'really serious harm' (see *DPP* v *Smith*) or more simply as 'serious harm' (see *R* v *Saunders*). Under the Joint Charging Standards, minor cuts would be charged as s.47 actual bodily harm or even as battery.

Mens rea

The main difference between sections 18 and 20 lies in the fault element, and it is a considerable difference. Section 20 requires either intention or recklessness to inflict some harm. This fault element was confirmed in the cases of *R* v *Mowatt* and *R* v *Grimshaw*, which held that there is no need to prove recklessness as to wounding or grievous bodily harm, so long as the court is satisfied that 'the defendant should have foreseen that some physical harm to some other person, albeit of a minor character, might result'. As in all non-fatal offences where the *mens rea* includes recklessness, this is 'Cunningham' or 'subjective' recklessness — the prosecution must prove that the defendant did recognise the risk he or she was running.

Wounding or causing grievous bodily harm with intent (to cause GBH) (s.18)

This is a serious offence which carries a maximum sentence of life imprisonment (compared with a maximum of 5 years under s.20). There are two forms of intent, the most common being 'with intent to cause grievous bodily harm'. Note that most serious injuries involve the use of a weapon, and this makes it easier to establish the necessary intent. This section requires proof that the defendant intended specifically to cause a serious injury (see *R* v *Nedrick* and *R* v *Woollin*). This is either direct intent, where the defendant's aim or objective was to cause grievous bodily harm, or oblique intent, where the jury is satisfied that the defendant foresaw serious injury as virtually certain. In most cases of s.18 grievous bodily harm, the defendant will have used some form of weapon to inflict injuries on the victim. Where the prosecution fails to establish intention, the offence is reduced to the lower s.20 offence, so long as recklessness is proved.

The alternative fault element is 'with intent to prevent the lawful apprehension of any person'. While the policy of this requirement is understandable — making attacks on persons engaged in law enforcement are regarded as more serious — under this head the defendant can be convicted if he or she pushes a police officer to prevent an arrest, and the officer falls and suffers a serious injury. There is no requirement that such serious results should have been foreseen or even foreseeable. It is, however, a requirement in such cases that the prosecution proves that the defendant intended some harm, or was reckless as to whether harm was caused.

Summary of non-fatal offences

Crime	Actus reus	Mens rea	Cases	Maximum sentence
Assault	Causing the victim to apprehend immediate, unlawful personal violence	Intention or subjective recklessness to causing *actus reus*	Logdon, Ireland, Constanza	6 months or £5,000 fine
Battery	Infliction of unlawful personal violence	Intention or subjective recklessness as to inflicting unlawful personal violence	Fagan, Thomas	6 months or £5,000 fine
Section 47 ABH	Assault or battery causing actual bodily harm	Intention or recklessness as to the assault or battery	Miller, Chan-Fook, Savage, Parmenter, Roberts	5 years
Section 20 GBH/ wounding	Wounding: all layers of skin must be broken; GBH: serious injury	Intention or recklessness as to *some* harm	Eisenhower, Smith, Mowatt, Grimshaw	5 years
Section 18 GBH with intent	Wounding or GBH as in s.20	Specific intent to cause GBH, or intent to resist lawful arrest	Nedrick, Woollin	Life

Joint Charging Standard

The following table, agreed by police and the Crown Prosecution Service, has been produced in order to clarify the offences which would normally be charged following different levels of injury. It is, however, important that you can also identify other potential offences which could be charged; for example, a minor cut or graze could potentially be charged as wounding.

Section 39 of the Criminal Justice Act: common assault (battery)	Section 47: assault occasioning ABH	Section 18 or Section 20: GBH or wounding
Grazes or scratches	Loss or breaking of tooth	Injury causing permanent disability or disfigurement
Abrasions	Temporary loss of consciousness	Broken limbs or bones
Minor bruising	Extensive or multiple bruising	Dislocated joints
Swellings	Displaced broken nose	Injuries causing substantial loss of blood
Reddening of the skin	Minor fractures	Injuries resulting in lengthy treatment
Superficial cuts	Minor cuts requiring stitches	
A black eye	Psychiatric injury — more than fear, distress or panic	

Murder

This is the most serious crime against the person. If convicted, the offender will receive a mandatory life sentence. Murder is defined as 'unlawful killing with malice aforethought'. The *actus reus* is unlawful killing and the *mens rea* — malice aforethought — is more clearly defined as intent to kill or commit grievous bodily harm.

Actus reus of murder: causation

The *actus reus* usually requires the examination of various rules of causation in order to establish whether the defendant caused or brought about the death of the victim. To be guilty of murder, the defendant must not only have attacked the victim in some way, but also have caused the victim to die.

The 'but for' rule

The first rule to be considered is the factual rule of causation, referred to as the 'but for' rule. This simply requires the prosecution to prove that 'but for' the defendant's act, the event would not have occurred. This is illustrated by the case of *R v White*, in which the defendant put potassium cyanide into a drink with intent to murder his mother. She was found dead shortly afterwards with the glass, three-quarters filled, beside her. However, the medical evidence showed that she had died, not of poison, but of heart failure. The defendant was acquitted of murder and convicted of attempted murder. Although the consequence that the defendant intended had occurred, he did not cause it to occur and therefore there was no *actus reus* of murder.

While it is usually easy to prove this 'but for' rule, there are many situations where the question of causation is much more difficult to establish clearly. A. M. Dugdale in *A-Level Law* (Butterworths, 3rd edn, 1996) lists some examples:

- A points a gun at B and B dies of a heart attack
- A knocks B unconscious and leaves him lying in a road where he is run over by a car and killed
- A injures B, who is being taken by ambulance to hospital when the ambulance crashes, killing all the occupants
- A knocks B unconscious and B remains lying in a street for several hours, where she is robbed, raped or further assaulted

In all of these examples, it could be argued that A caused the consequences, on the basis that none of these things would have happened 'but for' the initial attack by A on B. The difficulty with this approach, however, is that it can link an initial cause (the attack) with consequences that are both highly improbable and unforeseeable. This has been a particular problem in cases of unlawful killing — murder and manslaughter — in which there is a less direct link between act and effect. In such cases, one has to consider what the responsibility of the defendant is for the victim's death.

Significant contribution

At one time it was the legal position that the defendant was liable for all natural and probable consequences of his or her voluntary acts. This presumption has now been overturned on the grounds that it could link together events that are connected too remotely. In *R v Marjoram* the trial judge instructed the jury to consider the legal cause — there must be something which could reasonably be foreseen as a consequence of the unlawful act. Nowadays it is accepted law that the defendant needs only to have made 'a significant contribution' to the unlawful result, as seen in *R v Cheshire* (1991), or to have been an 'operative and substantial cause of harm'.

Another case exemplifying this principle is *R v Smith* (1959), where a fight between two soldiers resulted in the victim receiving a bayonet wound requiring medical treatment. While being carried to the medical reception station, the victim was dropped twice. The doctor failed to diagnose a punctured lung and gave treatment that was later described as 'thoroughly bad'. However, Smith was convicted of murder and his appeal failed. The key rule was that:

> ...if at the time of death the original wound is still the operating and substantial cause, then the death can be properly said to be the result of the wound, albeit some other cause of death is also operating. Only if it can be said that the original wound is merely the setting in which another cause operates can it be said that the death does not result from the wound.

This situation occurred in the case of *R v Jordan*, where the victim of a serious injury made a good recovery in hospital but while recuperating received an injection of a drug to which he was allergic. The doctors confirmed that his death was not caused by the original wound, which was mainly healed at the time of death, but by the injection (and also the intravenous introduction of large quantities of liquid). The defendant's conviction was therefore quashed on appeal.

Novus actus interveniens

A further issue that occurs in causation is what constitutes a new intervening act (*novus actus interveniens*). For such an act to invalidate the *actus reus*, it must be something which cannot be foreseen and is overwhelming. For example, A shoots at B and causes B serious internal injuries which could be treated successfully if immediate and specialised medical treatment is provided, but the ambulance takes 10 minutes to arrive and B dies. This is a foreseeable result and A is guilty of murder.

You should also consider 'escape cases', in which the victim has suffered injury or has been killed while trying to escape from a serious attack. In such cases, as established in *R v Roberts*, the defendant is liable if the victim's conduct in running away was within the range of foreseeable responses to the defendant's behaviour.

The 'thin skull' rule

The 'thin skull' rule, or 'take your victim as you find him', refers to the situation where the intervening cause is a pre-existing weakness of the victim, such as an abnormally thin skull. If, as a result of this weakness, a blow inflicted on the victim causes serious injury or even death, when in a 'normal' person it would usually only cause a bruise, the attacker is liable for the more serious injury or the death.

This rule covers not only physical but also mental conditions, and even the victim's beliefs or values, as in *R v Blaue*. Here the victim of a stabbing was a Jehovah's Witness, who refused on religious grounds to accept a blood transfusion which would have saved her life. The defendant was convicted of her manslaughter and the Court of Appeal rejected his appeal, holding that the victim's refusal to accept the transfusion did not break the causal chain.

Mens rea: malice aforethought — specific intent

The *mens rea* of murder is malice aforethought, which means intent to kill or commit grievous bodily harm. The meaning of 'intention' is not found in any statute, but in judicial decisions. It is clear that a person intends a result when it is his or her aim or objective or purpose to bring it about. This might be termed 'dictionary intention'.

However, the concept of intention is open to ambiguity. What is the position when someone has clearly caused an illegal result, realising that it will almost certainly occur although it was not his or her primary intention? There is a well-known hypothetical example of a person placing a bomb in an aircraft with the intention that it will explode when the plane reaches an altitude of 20,000 feet. His specific aim or objective is to obtain the insurance money on the value of the lost aircraft. In these circumstances he surely knows that when the plane explodes all the passengers and crew will be killed, but does he really intend their deaths? This type of case is one of 'oblique intent'.

Oblique intent

In the case of *R v Hancock and Shankland*, this issue was at the heart of the case — how the law should deal with the defendant who has committed an unlawful result, where it is clear that the outcome was probable, even highly probable, and the defendant may well have foreseen this outcome. The defendants in the case were Welsh coal miners on strike. When one of their fellow-miners wanted to return to work, they tried to stop the strike-breaker as he was being driven to another coal mine in a taxi. The route took them on to a motorway. When the taxi passed under a bridge, the striking miners threw down rocks and pieces of the bridge. One of the larger rocks smashed through the windscreen and killed the driver. Clearly the miners had killed the taxi driver and had they been charged with manslaughter would have pleaded guilty. However, the charge was murder, which requires there to be intention to kill or commit serious injury. The defendants denied having such an intention, admitting only that their intention was to prevent the strike-breaker reaching the coal mine.

Although they were convicted of murder at their trial, the Court of Appeal and House of Lords both quashed that conviction and substituted a manslaughter conviction, holding that the issue of intention had not been established. Lord Scarman indicated that, in cases like these, juries needed to be told by the judge that 'the greater the probability of a consequence occurring, the more likely it was so foreseen and, if so, the more likely it was intended'. This emphasised that foresight of a degree of probability was the only evidence from which intention could be inferred.

In the more recent cases of *R v Nedrick* and *R v Woollin* (see below), a tighter rule was laid down for such cases of oblique intent. This now requires juries to return a verdict of murder only where they find that 'the defendant foresaw death or serious injury as a virtually certain consequence of his or her voluntary actions'. It is worth pointing out that, in both these cases, the original murder conviction was changed on appeal to a manslaughter conviction.

R v Woollin (1998)

This case resulted from the death of a 3-month-old baby. Although initially the defendant gave a number of different explanations, he finally admitted that he 'had lost his cool' when his baby started to choke. He had shaken the baby and then, in a fit of rage or frustration, had thrown him in the direction of his pram which was standing against the wall some 3 or 4 feet away. He knew that the baby's head had hit something hard but denied intending to throw him against the wall or wanting him to die or to suffer serious injury. The trial judge directed the members of jury that they might infer intention if they were satisfied that when he threw the baby, the defendant appreciated there was a 'substantial risk' of causing serious harm. In the Court of Appeal, the defendant argued that the judge should have used the words 'virtual certainty', as 'substantial risk' was merely a test of recklessness. The Court of Appeal, although critical of the trial judge, dismissed the appeal, and certified questions for the House of Lords. The House of Lords quashed the defendant's conviction for murder and substituted a conviction for manslaughter.

Lord Steyn gave the main speech, saying that 'a result foreseen as virtually certain is an intended result'. Thus the phrase 'substantial risk' used by the trial judge blurred the distinction between intention and recklessness, and was too serious a misdirection for the conviction to stand.

> **Tip**
>
> If the fatal offence question requires you to consider whether a particular killing is to be dealt with as homicide (all kinds of unlawful killing) rather than murder or manslaughter, the choice of whether to answer in terms of murder or manslaughter can only be made by deciding whether the defendant killed with intent — either direct or oblique. If there was intent, you should consider murder; if there was no intent, your answer should be about involuntary manslaughter.

Voluntary manslaughter

Voluntary manslaughter is unique in that it is the only offence for which a defendant can be convicted but not charged. This situation arises out of a murder charge, when the defendant has committed the *actus reus* of unlawful killing with the requisite *mens rea* required of specific intent to kill or commit grievous bodily harm. However, one of the following extenuating circumstances operates as a **partial defence**, all of which are now contained in the **Homicide Act 1957**:

- diminished responsibility (s.2)

- provocation (s.3)
- suicide pact (s.4)

The justification for the existence of the voluntary manslaughter offence is the problem caused by the imposition of the mandatory life sentence for murder. The basis of all serious criminal liability — liability to be prosecuted and, if convicted, to be punished — rests on the principle of fault. These partial defences, which can only be pleaded to a murder charge, recognise that the defendant's fault has been reduced in some way and therefore he or she is entitled to receive a lesser punishment. Partial defences were even more important before 1963 than they are today because the mandatory penalty for murder was hanging. In a sense, these defences operated as 'gallows savers'.

The extent to which both diminished responsibility and provocation have been widened in the scope of their operation is outlined below. This is especially true of provocation, where cases such as *Morhall* and *Smith* have to a large extent challenged the objectivity of the reasonable person test.

Diminished responsibility

Section 2 of the Homicide Act states:

> ...where a person kills, he shall not be convicted of murder if he was suffering from such abnormality of mind (whether arising from a condition of arrested or retarded development, or induced by disease or injury) as substantially impaired his mental responsibility for his acts or omissions in doing or being a party to the killing.

This partial defence was introduced into English law from Scots law, where in *HM Advocate* v *Braithwaite* Lord President Cooper defined the defendant's state of mind as 'bordering on but not amounting to insanity'.

Another leading case is that of *R* v *Byrne*, where the defendant suffered from perverted sexual desires which created impulses that he found impossible to control. Here Lord Parker CJ stated: '...an abnormality of mind is a state of mind so different from that of ordinary human beings that the reasonable man would term it abnormal.' He went on to stress that, once the jury is satisfied that the defendant is suffering from an abnormality of mind, they must be satisfied that this abnormality was 'significant enough to substantially impair his mental responsibility for his acts'. The impairment of control need not be complete, but it must be considerable. In *Byrne* there was evidence that the impulses from which the defendant suffered were not absolutely irresistible, but extremely difficult to control. This was considered sufficient, but it will always be a matter for the jury to decide.

The required abnormality of mind has been held to cover severe shock or depression, especially in cases of mercy killing. In 1997 the Court of Appeal accepted that 'battered woman's syndrome' was a mental disease and could thus cause an abnormality of mind.

Note that, as for the defence of insanity, the burden of proof rests with the defendant to prove both elements of this defence, but at the civil standard of proof — i.e. on the balance of probabilities.

Intoxication and diminished responsibility

The crucial point here is the effect of the alcohol. If alcohol has produced an abnormality of the mind — for example, the brain has been damaged because the defendant is an alcoholic — then the defence could be established. However, the transitory effect of drink on the mind would not be a defence. In the case of *R* v *Tandy* it was held that, for drink to produce an abnormality of mind, the 'alcoholism had to have reached such a level that the defendant's brain was damaged so that there was gross impairment of his judgment and emotional responses or the craving for drink had to be such as to render the defendant's use of drink involuntary because he was no longer able to resist the impulse to drink'.

In the case of *R* v *Dietschmann* (2003), the defendant had killed the victim while intoxicated and also while suffering from an abnormality of mind, but there was no evidence to establish alcohol dependency as an abnormality of mind. It was found that if a defendant satisfies the jury that, notwithstanding the alcohol he or she has consumed and its effect upon him/her, his/her abnormality of mind substantially impaired his/her mental responsibility for his/her acts in doing the killing, the jury should find him/her not guilty of murder, but guilty of voluntary manslaughter by reason of diminished responsibility.

Section 2 does not require abnormality of mind to be the sole cause of the defendant's acts in doing the killing. Therefore, even if the defendant would not have killed if he had not taken drink, the causative effect of the drink does not necessarily prevent an abnormality of mind suffered by him from substantially impairing his mental responsibility for his fatal acts.

The cases of *R* v *Atkinson* and *R* v *Egan* were therefore wrongly decided, because they held that a defence of diminished responsibility is available only if the defendant can show that he or she would have killed even if he or she had not taken drink. A jury should be directed that drink cannot be taken into account as a factor which contributed to the mental impairment within s.2 and to any impairment of mental responsibility arising from that abnormality. However, a defendant should be convicted of voluntary manslaughter on the grounds of diminished responsibility if he or she can satisfy the jury that, despite the drink, his or her mental abnormality substantially impaired his or her mental responsibility for the fatal acts. For more information on this defence, see pages 37–38.

Tip

Do not refer to the defence of diminished responsibility except in murder cases, where the possibility of insanity (see pp. 33–35) should also be considered.

Provocation

The reduced fault may be established through provocation, where the defendant alleges that he or she lost self-control because of provocation and that 'the reasonable man' would also have lost self-control and reacted by killing. Section 3 of the Homicide Act states:

> Where on a charge of murder there is evidence on which a jury can find that the defendant was provoked (whether by things done or said or both) to lose their self-control, the question whether the provocation was enough to make a reasonable man do as he did shall be left to be determined by the jury; and in determining that question, the jury shall take into account everything both done and said according to the effect which, in their opinion, it would have on a reasonable man.

Proving provocation

The criteria for establishing provocation, together with the supporting cases, are outlined below.

(1) Evidence presented
There must be evidence capable of amounting to provocation. This is decided by the judge and is the limit of the judge's role, as the success or failure of the defence is left to the jury. Note that even if this defence has not been presented specifically by the defence, if there is some evidence of provocation it must be put by the judge to the jury (*R* v *Cambridge*). In the case of *R* v *Acott*, it was held that as there was no specific evidence that the defendant was provoked but merely speculation, the trial judge was right not to direct the jury on the issue of provocation.

(2) Verbal and physical provocation
Provocation may result from things said or done or both. Prior to the Homicide Act, only things done could amount in law to provocation.

(3) Loss of self-control
The provocation must have caused the defendant to lose his or her self-control. If the defendant, although provoked, lost his or her self-control for any other reason, the defence falls. In *R* v *Duffy*, Lord Devlin defined the effect of provocation as 'a sudden and temporary loss of self-control, rendering the defendant so subject to passion as to make him for the moment not the master of his mind'. Note that evidence of provocation followed by premeditated action will result in this defence being lost, as in *R* v *Ibrams*, where it was held that the existence of a 'cooling-off period' between the provocation and the killing was evidence that the loss of self-control was not 'sudden and temporary'. However, the existence of a 'cooling-off period' is not a matter of law but a piece of evidence that the jury may use to decide whether, at the time of the killing, the defendant was deprived of self-control (see *R* v *Ahluwalia*). Note that, in considering provocation, a court can take into account

the cumulative provocation that has taken place over a long period of time (see *R* v *Humphrey*).

(4) Induced provocation

Following *R* v *Johnson* (1989), it has been established that if the defendant induced the provocation in the first place this does not necessarily prevent the defence being available. In this case, the defendant and his male friend had been drinking, and the defendant threatened violence towards his friend and his friend's female companion. A struggle took place between the defendant and his friend, during which the defendant stabbed his friend to death with a flick-knife. His appeal against his murder conviction was allowed, because the judge had refused to allow the issue of provocation to be considered by the jury. However, it seems to be the law in such cases that the provocation suffered by the defendant must be extreme in comparison with the defendant's original act (of provocation).

(5) The 'reasonable man' test

For the defence to succeed, it must be proved not only that a 'reasonable man' would have been provoked, but that such provocation would have made a 'reasonable man' act as the defendant did — in other words, that the response was not out of all proportion to the provocation. The case of *R* v *Bedder* was overruled by *DPP* v *Camplin*, in which Lord Diplock stated that the 'reasonable man' 'is a person having the power of self-control to be expected of an ordinary person of the sex and age of the defendant, but in other respects sharing such of the defendant's characteristics as they think would affect the gravity of the provocation to him'.

This definition of the 'reasonable man' was applied in *R* v *Roberts*, where a 23-year-old man suffering from substantial deafness and impaired speech killed someone as a result of taunts about his condition. It was held that the judge had rightly directed that the hypothetical 'reasonable man' had the impairments of the defendant. Both *Ahluwalia* and *Thornton* have now confirmed that 'battered woman's syndrome' might constitute a relevant characteristic.

Objectivity

The objective test of provocation has been stretched considerably by two important cases. In *R* v *Morhall*, the defendant was a glue-sniffer who was taunted by the victim about his addiction. A fight ensued in which the defendant killed the other man. He was convicted of murder and appealed on the grounds that he fell within the defence of provocation. The Court of Appeal rejected his submission on the grounds that 'repugnant characteristics' could not be attributed to the 'reasonable man'. However, the House of Lords overturned the Court of Appeal's judgment, holding that such characteristics could and should be taken into account when applying the objective 'reasonable man' test, provided that the characteristic was the target of the provocation. It had to be the 'response' characteristic that was attributed to the 'reasonable man', as opposed to the 'control' characteristics, which merely have an effect on the defendant's ability to control him or herself (see *Luc Thiet Thuan*, itself overturned by

R v *Smith*). This distinction was identified by Andrew Ashworth in 'The doctrine of provocation' (*The Cambridge Law Journal*, 1976), where he asserted that 'the proper distinction is that individual peculiarities which bear on the gravity of the provocation should be taken into account, whereas individual peculiarities bearing on the accused's level of self-control should not'.

Following *R* v *Smith*, the objective nature of the 'reasonable man' test appears to have largely disappeared, as has the distinction between 'response' and 'control' characteristics. In this case the defendant and his victim had been friends for a long time, but the defendant had become unhappy about seeing the victim socially because of a number of incidents. When the victim visited the defendant, an argument began as to whether the victim had taken some of the defendant's tools and had sold them to buy drink. The argument became heated and the defendant stabbed the victim several times with a kitchen knife, killing him. At the defendant's trial for murder, his plea of diminished responsibility was based on his suffering from a depressive illness which might have reduced his threshold for erupting with violence and might have disinhibited him. The trial judge ruled that this characteristic was relevant only to the gravity of the provocation and not to the 'reasonable man's' ability to maintain self-control. The defendant was convicted of murder.

However, both the Court of Appeal and the House of Lords accepted the defendant's argument that decisions in *Ahluwalia*, *Humphrey* and *Thornton (no. 2)* favoured a more flexible approach to the 'reasonable man' test, so the trial judge's ruling was incorrect. The conviction was reduced to manslaughter. It was further held that there was nothing in *Camplin* (see p. 24) to support the distinction between characteristics relevant only to the gravity of the provocation and those relevant to loss of control. Lord Hoffman stated:

> In my opinion, judges should not be required to describe the objective element in the provocation defence by reference to a reasonable man, with or without attribution of personal characteristics (of the defendant). They may instead find it more helpful to explain in simple language the principles of the doctrine of provocation. First, it requires that the defendant should have killed while he had lost self-control (as a result of provocation). Secondly, the fact that something caused him to lose self-control is not enough. The law expects people to exercise control over their emotions. A tendency to violent rages or childish tantrums is a defect in character rather than an excuse. The jury must think that the circumstances were such as to make the loss of self-control sufficiently excusable to reduce the gravity of the offence from murder to manslaughter. This is entirely a question for the jury.
>
> The general principle is that the same standards of behaviour are expected of everyone, regardless of their individual psychological make-up. In most cases, nothing more will need to be said. But the jury should, in an appropriate case, be told that this is a principle and not a rigid rule. It may sometimes have to yield to a more important principle, which is to do justice in the particular case. So the jury may think that there was some characteristic of the defendant, whether temporary

or permanent, which affected the degree of control which society could reasonably have expected of him and which it would be unjust not to take into account.

In an article in the *New Law Journal* on 11 August 2000, Laurence Toczek writes:

> Lord Hoffman attempts to deal with the argument that if there is no limit to the characteristics which can be taken into account, the objective element will disappear completely. Lord Hoffman agrees that this would be most undesirable. His solution is to suggest that judges should direct juries that 'characteristics such as jealousy and obsession should be ignored in relation to the objective element' (Lord Clyde adds 'exceptional pugnacity or excitability' to this list of excluded characteristics).

As Toczek points out, this creates an obvious problem: 'how is the line to be drawn between inadmissible characteristics of this sort and admissible characteristics such as Smith's depressive illness?'

Finally, note that for reasons of policy, intoxication cannot be taken into account because of the common law rule (see *R* v *Newell*) that intoxication does not of itself excuse a man from committing a criminal offence.

Suicide pact

Section 4 of the Homicide Act states that a person who kills another in pursuance of a suicide pact is guilty of manslaughter, not murder. According to Andrew Ashworth: '...a suicide pact exists where two or more people, each having a settled intention of dying, reach an agreement which has as its object the death of both or of all' (*Principles of Criminal Law*, OUP, 1999). This is extremely rare and in fact there are no reported cases.

Involuntary manslaughter

This category includes all types of homicide (unlawful killing) that are committed without malice aforethought — that is, without specific intent to kill or to commit grievous bodily harm. Involuntary manslaughter has always been the most difficult kind of homicide to define because of its negative definition of *mens rea*. Lord Atkin has observed:

> ...of all crimes manslaughter appears to afford most difficulties of definition, for it concerns homicide in so many and so varying conditions...the law...recognises murder on the one hand based mainly, though not exclusively, on an intention to kill, and manslaughter on the other hand, based mainly, though not exclusively, on the absence of intent to kill, but with the presence of an element of 'unlawfulness' which is the elusive factor.

A further source of difficulty is that manslaughter is situated between murder at the extreme end of criminal liability and accidental death at the other end, where no criminal liability usually attaches.

At the present time, the law recognises two broad categories of involuntary manslaughter:
- unlawful and dangerous act manslaughter
- gross negligence manslaughter

Unlawful and dangerous act manslaughter

This offence is also known as Church doctrine manslaughter, after a leading case. The requirements are as follows:

> ...a defendant is guilty of manslaughter if he kills by an unlawful and dangerous act. The only *mens rea* required is an intention (or recklessness) to do that act. It is irrelevant that the defendant is unaware that it is unlawful or that it is dangerous, if a reasonable person would have been aware of it.

Unlawful act

It is now established that, for the purposes of this offence, for the act to be 'unlawful' it must be a crime — a tort or breach of contract is not enough. In *R v Franklin*, which involved the tort of trespass, the trial judge ruled that the 'mere fact of a civil wrong committed by one person against another ought not to be used as an incident which is a necessary step in a criminal case'. This crime must be identified and proved, including the necessary *mens rea* (see *R v Lamb* and *R v Jennings*). Lamb's conviction was quashed on appeal because no initial crime was proved to have been committed. In *R v Scarlett* the defendant's conviction was overturned because the Crown had not been able to produce evidence that the use of force by the defendant had been unreasonable and therefore unlawful.

It is vital to understand that the *mens rea* for involuntary manslaughter concerns the initial crime itself, and can be intention or recklessness. Although most cases involve some form of assault that requires intention or subjective recklessness, in *DPP v Newbury and Jones* the initial offence (which was not identified in the case) was surely that of criminal damage, for which Caldwell or objective recklessness was formerly required. However, following *R v G* (2003), this kind of recklessness is no longer applicable.

As regards the issue of omission, it seems that, following *R v Lowe*, if the omission is no more than an act of negligence it will not be the basis of unlawful and dangerous act manslaughter. Omissions that cause death should be dealt with under the law on gross negligence manslaughter. However, if the omission is truly wilful (for example, a deliberate omission to summon emergency medical aid, knowing it to be necessary), the offence should be treated as unlawful and dangerous act manslaughter.

Dangerous act

In *R v Church*, Lord Edmund-Davies stated:

> For such a verdict to follow, the unlawful act must be such as all sober and reasonable people would inevitably recognise must subject the other person to, at least, the risk of some harm resulting therefrom, albeit not serious harm.

The test of dangerousness is therefore objective. In *Newbury*, Lord Salmon stressed that 'the test is not that the defendant recognised that it was dangerous but would all sober and reasonable people recognise its danger'. This extends the test to consider whether the 'reasonable man' would have appreciated that the act was dangerous, not only in the light of the circumstances actually known to the defendant, but also of any additional circumstances of which the hypothetical person would have been aware. Refer to *R v Watson*, but note that the conviction for the manslaughter of an 87-year-old man during a burglary was later overturned on appeal, on the grounds that causation had not been proved.

R v Dawson concerned an armed robbery at a petrol station that led to the death of the attendant from a heart attack. The original conviction for manslaughter was quashed on appeal because the court apparently assumed that, in the context of this offence, 'harm' includes 'injury to the person through the operation of shock emanating from fright'. As Professor J. C. Smith comments in *Criminal Law* (Butterworths, 7th edn, 1992), '...it seems that it is not enough that the act is likely to frighten. It must be likely to cause such shock as to result in physical injury.' The question also arises as to why the 'thin skull' rule was not applied in this case.

Causation

The unlawful and dangerous act must be the cause of the victim's death. At one time it was considered that the act had to be directed at the victim, but following *R v Goodfellow* it is now clear that if the act satisfies the normal factual and legal rules of causation this will suffice for a charge of manslaughter to be brought. This decision was confirmed by the House of Lords in *Attorney-General's Reference (No. 3 of 1994)*, where it was not only held that there is no requirement for the unlawful act to be directed at the victim, but that there is no requirement that the danger or risk of harm be directed at the actual victim. A risk of harm to someone else arising from the unlawful and dangerous act will suffice.

Gross negligence manslaughter

This type of manslaughter is based on the civil tort of negligence and is most commonly the result of an omission — a failure to act where there is a clear duty to act (see *R v Stone and Dobinson*). The opinion expressed by Lord Hewart CJ in *R v Bateman* is still important:

In order to establish criminal liability the fact must be such that in the opinion of the jury, the negligence of the accused went beyond a mere matter of compensation between subjects (civil tort liability) and showed such disregard for the life and safety of others as to amount to a crime against the state and conduct deserving punishment.

The rules which the Crown is obliged to satisfy to obtain a conviction for gross negligence manslaughter are given below.

(1) Duty of care owed by the defendant to the victim

Defining duty of care

This issue has caused considerable difficulty but, following *R* v *Adomako*, it now appears that duty of care is based simply on the 'neighbour' test in *Donoghue* v *Stevenson* or the incremental approach in *Caparo* v *Dickman*. The test is therefore whether it was reasonably foreseeable that the victim would be injured.

However, the more recent case of *R* v *Singh* (1999) laid down the current rule whereby 'the circumstances must be such that a reasonably prudent person would have foreseen a serious and obvious risk not merely of injury or even of serious injury but of death'. In this case, the victim was a tenant who died of carbon monoxide poisoning and this death was foreseeable by the landlord's son, who was in charge of maintenance. This case also made it clear that the question of whether a duty of care exists is a matter of law to be decided by the trial judge. Professor Smith commented: 'It seems that the deliberate taking of a high degree of risk of causing serious bodily harm which results in death (formerly murder under *Hyam* v *DPP*) must now be manslaughter....'

This requires the risk in respect of which the defendant was negligent to have been one of death rather than any lesser degree of harm. It clarifies one of the major problems with the speech of Lord Mackay LC in *R* v *Adomako* (see below), which was a lack of definition as to the extent of risk. However, if the defendant is reckless as to a lesser degree of harm but does cause the victim's death, this may amount to reckless manslaughter. This is a category of manslaughter that Lord Mackay left open and which forms the focus of considerable academic speculation, although it does not feature in the law reports.

Examples of duty of care situations

These could include doctor–patient and landlord–tenant. In *R* v *Becker*, the defendant was a doctor on emergency call who attended the victim at his home. The victim was suffering from severe pain resulting from a kidney stone and the defendant prescribed a painkiller, having made a correct diagnosis. However, the painkiller did not work quickly enough and the defendant decided to prescribe an opiate as well. Although the victim indicated that the pain had eased, the defendant went ahead with an injection of 30mg of diamorphine. The victim died later that day from the overdose. The defendant was convicted of gross negligence manslaughter after a trial in which it was common ground that the injection of that quantity of the drug (about three times the largest permissible dose) was conduct falling below the standard expected of a reasonably competent GP. The sole issue for the jury was whether this amounted to gross negligence.

You should be aware that cases such as *R v Khan* and *R v Lewin* suggest that judges are reluctant to extend the areas where there could be a duty of care. The *Khan* case involved a defendant who was a pimp and gave heroin to a prostitute, leaving her when it was clear that she was in a coma from which she later died. *Lewin* involved a defendant who was a friend of the victim and left him in a car after a heavy drinking session in Marbella.

(2) Breach of duty of care that causes the death of the victim

The test for breach of duty is again the tort test. The defendant's conduct must have been below the standard expected of a reasonable person. The various 'risk' factors should then be considered — the probability of harm, the seriousness of the injury, etc. You should also note the second part of this rule, which is that the breach must have caused death. In your answers you should mention, even briefly, both the factual 'but for' rule and the legal rules of causation.

(3) Gross negligence

This is the *mens rea* for the offence of gross negligence manslaughter. As can be seen from the statement by Lord Hewart CJ, quoted above, its presence is for the members of the jury to decide. They must consider whether, regarding the risk of death involved, the conduct of the defendant was so bad in all the circumstances as to amount in their judgment to a criminal act or omission.

R v Adomako

In the case of *R v Adomako*, Lord Taylor CJ indicated that 'gross negligence' could include the following:
- indifference to an obvious risk of injury to health
- actual foresight of the risk coupled with the determination nevertheless to run it
- an appreciation of the risk coupled with an intention to avoid it, but also coupled with such a high degree of negligence in the attempted avoidance that the jury considered a conviction to be justified
- inattention or failure to address a serious risk, which went beyond 'mere inadvertence' in respect of an obvious and important matter that the defendant's duty demanded he or she should address

The defendant was an anaesthetist who, during an eye operation, failed to notice that the patient's breathing tube had become disconnected. In the 6 minutes that elapsed from the time of the disconnection, the defendant did not notice the patient turning blue through anoxia or the gas gauges on the anaesthetic machine oscillating wildly; he even ignored the audible warning signal that the machine emitted. This case was appealed in the House of Lords, which effectively returned this branch of the law to the traditional rules of gross negligence manslaughter laid down in *Bateman* and *Andrews* after a 'wrong turn' had been taken in both *R* v *Lawrence* and *R* v *Seymour*. *Lawrence* had created reckless manslaughter by extending Caldwell objective recklessness to manslaughter, and *Seymour* had created motor manslaughter.

General defences

Unit 4 usually requires candidates to consider the possible defences that may be available to a defendant charged with an offence against the person, as well as explaining the *actus reus* and *mens rea* of the offence. You therefore need to learn these defences and be able to apply them in problem-solving questions. The Question and Answer section of this guide will help you to do this.

Insanity

The M'Naghten rules

According to the M'Naghten rules, which originated from *R* v *M'Naghten* (1843), to establish a defence on the grounds of insanity it must be clearly proved that at the time of the committing of the act 'the party accused was labouring under such a defect of reason, from disease of the mind, as not to know the nature and quality of the act he was doing, or, if he did know it, he did not know that what he was doing was wrong'.

Two lines of defence are therefore open:
- The defendant must be acquitted if, because of a disease of the mind, he or she did not know the nature or quality of the act.
- Even if the defendant did know the nature or quality of the act, the defendant must be acquitted if, because of a disease of the mind, he or she did not know it was 'wrong'.

After the introduction of the partial defence of diminished responsibility under s.2 of the Homicide Act 1957 (see pp. 21–22) this defence was rarely used. However, in the 5 years following the introduction of the **Criminal Procedure (Insanity) Act 1991** there were 44 findings of 'not guilty by reason of insanity'. Michael Allen in *Elliott and Wood's Cases and Materials on Criminal Law* (Sweet and Maxwell, 8th edn, 2001) suggests that this increase in the use of insanity as a defence can be attributed to 'an appreciation that the 1991 Act has removed the more glaring disincentives (such as automatic removal to a secure mental hospial) inherent within the 1964 Criminal Procedure (Insanity) Act'.

Disease of the mind
J. C. Smith and B. Hogan in *Criminal Law* (Butterworths, 7th edn, 1992) write:

> When a defendant puts his state of mind in issue, the question of whether he has raised the defence of insanity is one of law for the judge. Whether the defendant, or indeed his medical witnesses, would call the condition on which he relies 'insanity' is immaterial. The expert witnesses may testify as to the factual nature of the condition but it is for the judge to say whether that is evidence of a 'defect of reason from disease of the mind' because these are legal, not medical, concepts.

It seems that any disease which produces a malfunctioning of the mind, such as arteriosclerosis, a brain tumour, epilepsy and diabetes, is a disease of the mind. All physical diseases may amount in law to a disease of the mind if they produce the relevant malfunction. A malfunctioning of the mind is not, however, a disease of the mind when it is caused by some external factor, such as a blow on the head causing concussion, the consumption of alcohol or drugs etc. In *Bratty* v *Attorney-General for Northern Ireland*, Lord Denning used the following definition: '...it seems to me that any mental disorder which has manifested itself in violence and is prone to recur is a disease of the mind.'

In *R* v *Kemp* the defendant, who was suffering from arteriosclerosis, made a savage attack on his wife with a hammer. It was contended in court that his defect of reason arose from a purely physical condition and not from a disease of the mind. It was argued that, if a physical disease caused the brain cells to degenerate, then it would be a disease of the mind, but until this effect occurred it was a temporary interference with the working of the brain which was not unlike concussion and not a disease of the mind. Justice Devlin rejected this argument and ruled that the defendant was suffering from a disease of the mind:

> The law is not concerned with the brain but with the mind, in the sense that 'mind' is ordinarily used, the mental faculties of reason, memory and understanding...In my judgment the condition of the brain is irrelevant and so is the question of whether the condition of the mind is curable or incurable, transitory or permanent.

Defect of reason
Defect of reason is the basis of the M'Naghten rules. The disease of the mind must have given rise to a defect of reason. This means that the powers of reasoning must be impaired — a mere failure to use powers of reasoning that one has does not come within the rule. In *R* v *Clarke* (1972) the defendant claimed that she had taken articles from a supermarket without paying for them because of absentmindedness resulting from depression. However, it was held that, even if she was suffering from a disease of the mind, she had not raised the defence of insanity but was simply denying that she had *mens rea*.

The nature and quality of the act
This concerns the physical rather than the moral nature of the act, for example a man who cut a woman's throat believing he was cutting a loaf of bread, a nurse throwing

a baby into the fire thinking it was a log, and so on. Such persons who would kill in such circumstances under these delusions could not be convicted of murder, because they would lack the required *mens rea*.

Knowledge that the act was wrong

It is established law that, even if the defendant did not know that his or her action was against the law, the defendant will still be liable if he or she knew it was wrong 'according to the ordinary standard adopted by reasonable men'. In the case of *R* v *Windle* the defendant killed his wife, who was certifiably insane and who frequently spoke of committing suicide. He then phoned the police and when he was arrested, said: 'I suppose they will hang me for this.' At his trial, the defence of insanity was not allowed to be put before the jury because the words that the defendant used indicated that he knew killing his wife was legally wrong.

Automatism

Automatism is recognised as a defence to all crimes. It refers to situations where the defendant's actions are involuntary, in the sense that they are beyond his or her control. Typical examples are sleepwalking, acts done in a hypnotic trance, reflex actions and convulsions.

The rationale for the defence of automatism is quite clear. The defendant in such a situation is not responsible for the consequences of his or her actions. The act is, in a sense, not his or her own. The defendant does not deserve to be punished, nor would punishment serve any useful or rational purpose.

A good example of automatism is provided by *Hill* v *Baxter* (1958), where a driver lost control of his vehicle as he instinctively tried to fend off a swarm of bees that had entered the car through an open window. The response to this kind of stimulus is an automatic one — a reflex response — and it is easy to sustain the argument that the defendant should not be held liable for the consequences resulting from the loss of control of his car.

Although automatism has been referred to as a 'defence', the legally accurate analysis is that voluntariness is a basic ingredient of criminal liability. The onus, therefore, is on the prosecution to prove beyond reasonable doubt that the conduct of the defendant was voluntary. Note that the prosecution, however, is obliged to prove that the acts of the defendant were voluntary only if the defendant has laid an evidential foundation (generally of a medical type) that he or she was an automaton at the relevant time. Lord Denning in *Bratty* v *Attorney-General for Northern Ireland* stated:

> The requirement that it should be a voluntary act is essential...in every criminal case. No act is punishable if it is done involuntarily; and an involuntary act in this context — some people prefer to speak of it as 'automatism' — means an act which

is done by the muscles without any control by the mind such as a spasm, a reflex action or a convulsion; or an act done by a person who is not conscious of what he is doing such as an act done while suffering from concussion or whilst sleep-walking.

He went on to stress that an act is not to be regarded as involuntary if the person was conscious but nevertheless could not control his or her actions (irresistible impulse) or if he or she could not remember after the event exactly what had taken place.

In *Broome v Perkins* (1987) the defendant had been charged with driving without due care and attention. He drove a vehicle erratically for some 6 miles. It was held that even though there was some evidence to establish that he was suffering from hypoglycaemia (low blood sugar), the defendant must have been exercising conscious control of the vehicle, albeit imperfectly, in order to have manoeuvred the vehicle reasonably successfully over such a distance. You should also refer to *Attorney-General's Reference (No. 2) (1992)*, where the defence of 'partial awareness' was disallowed by the Court of Appeal.

Note that both of these cases emphasised the need for total loss of control, although in its draft Criminal Code the Law Commission suggested that effective loss of control would suffice. In addition, where the defendant is or becomes aware that he or she might lose conscious control of his or her actions, the defence of automatism is likely to be rejected by the jury, assuming that an adequate evidential foundation has been laid.

Insane and non-insane automatism

If the automatism results from a 'disease of the mind' as defined under the M'Naghten rules, the condition amounts to what is legally termed insanity. In such circumstances the defendant is entitled only to a qualified acquittal by the special verdict of 'not guilty by reason of insanity', and the judge must make one of various orders under the Criminal Procedure (Insanity) Act 1991.

In *Bratty v Attorney-General for Northern Ireland* it was held, following *R v Kemp* (see p. 32), that if the defendant leads evidence of automatism, the prosecution is allowed to lead evidence that the condition giving rise to the automatism is a 'disease of the mind' and that the defendant is entitled only to a qualified acquittal. If the trial judge concludes, on the evidence, that the condition is a disease of the mind, he or she is entitled to refuse to let the defence of non-insane automatism go to the jury. In these circumstances the judge must instruct the jury that insanity is the only defence available to the defendant.

Any condition that impairs the functioning of the mind may amount to a 'disease of the mind'. It does not matter if the cause of the impairment is organic, as in epilepsy, or functional, as in schizophrenia. Nor does it matter if the impairment is permanent or transient and intermittent, provided that it was operative at the time of the alleged offence (*Sullivan*).

However, in *Bratty* Lord Denning gave a variation of this, stating that any condition that has 'manifested itself in violence and is prone to recur is a disease of the mind'. This reflects what many regard as the central policy underlying the insanity defence: to allow control (through compulsory treatment in a mental hospital) of those who, although not criminally responsible for the harm caused, are perceived to be suffering from a condition that makes them 'dangerous'.

If, however, the malfunctioning of the mind is caused by an external factor such as a blow to the head, alcohol or drugs, the condition does not constitute a disease of the mind. Compare the cases of *Quick*, a hypoglycaemic diabetic, and *Sullivan*, an epileptic whose defence of automatism was ruled to be one of insanity, and who then changed his plea to guilty. A distinction is made between hyperglycaemia, which is caused when a diabetic fails to take insulin, and hypoglycaemia, which is a result of failing to eat after taking insulin or taking too much insulin. Hyperglycaemia is regarded as internally caused (by the diabetes itself) and is therefore a 'disease of the mind' (*Hennessy*); hypoglycaemia is regarded as externally caused and amounts to non-insane automatism.

Consent

Consent has limited and controlled applications and it is important to remember how restricted this defence actually is. Indeed, the general rule for non-fatal crimes is that consent is not a defence. The Court of Appeal in *Attorney-General's Reference (No.6) (1980)* declared that where two persons fight, the blows inflicted can amount to a battery and the unlawfulness cannot be denied by pleading that the other party consented to the fight. Lord Lane CJ stated:

> It is not in the public interest that people should try to cause each other bodily harm for no good reason. Minor struggles are another matter. So, in our judgment, it is immaterial whether the act occurs in private or in public; it is an assault if actual bodily harm is intended and/or caused. This means that most fights will be unlawful regardless of consent.

This confirms the view taken by Justice Swift in *R v Donovan* (1934), when he stated that 'it is an unlawful act to beat another person with such a degree of violence that the infliction of bodily harm is a probable consequence, and when such an act is proved, consent is immaterial'.

Genuine consent

The first general rule is that the consent must be established as being genuine. In *R v Richardson* the defendant was a registered dentist who had been suspended from practice by the General Dental Council. While suspended she carried out dentistry on a number of patients, one of whom complained to the police. A prosecution was brought for actual bodily harm and the defendant was convicted. On appeal she argued that she had the defence of consent, as the complainant had consented to the treatment. The appeal was allowed.

However, a potentially broader interpretation of genuine consent was taken in *R* v *Tabassum*. In this case it was held that if the victim did not know the quality of the act carried out by the defendant, there has not been genuine consent.

Circumstances of consent

The next rule is that consent may only be pleaded to the crimes of assault and battery, and not to any more serious crime, unless the circumstances fall under the categories described below.

Sporting activities involving physical contact

In a number of sporting activities, such as rugby, football and hockey, physical contact is effectively part of the sport. In these cases, players are deemed to have consented even to serious injuries, provided these occur while the players are acting within the rules of the game (see *R* v *Billinghurst*).

Rough horseplay

In *R* v *Jones* a gang of schoolboys threw their victims up to 10 feet into the air, with the result that one victim suffered a ruptured spleen and broke his arm. The defence of consent was allowed on the basis that there was no intention to cause injury and, on appeal, convictions for grievous bodily harm were quashed. Another case to illustrate this exception is *R* v *Richardson and Irwin*, where the first defendant, the second defendant, the victim and others were university students who had been out drinking. On return to their accommodation, they indulged in horseplay as on previous occasions. This culminated in the victim being lifted over the edge of a balcony, from where he was dropped and fell about 10 feet. He suffered serious injuries and both the defendants were charged with and convicted of an s.20 offence. The Court of Appeal quashed their convictions because the trial judge confused subjective and objective recklessness in his direction to the jury. More importantly, the court held that:
- where the defendant pleads voluntary intoxication in response to an offence of basic intent, the Crown must prove that the defendant would have foreseen the risk had he not been intoxicated
- a mistaken belief by the defendant that the victim was consenting to run the risk of personal injury would enable the defendant to avoid liability, even if that mistake was induced by intoxication

Surgery including tattooing and body piercing

In the curious case of *R* v *Wilson*, the defendant had, at his wife's request, used a hot knife to brand his initials onto her bottom. The scars were found during a medical examination and he was subsequently charged with s.47 actual bodily harm. At his trial it was argued that his wife had consented to his conduct but the judge ruled (following *R* v *Brown*, the sado-masochistic case) that this defence was not available on these facts.

However, the Court of Appeal allowed the defendant's appeal on the basis that the case fell within the exception of tattooing recognised by *Brown*. The court also distinguished this case from *Brown* on the grounds that Mrs Wilson had not only consented to the branding but actually instigated it, and there was clearly no aggressive intent on the part of the husband. The court finally ruled, through Russell LJ, that 'consensual activity between husband and wife, in the privacy of the matrimonial home, is not, in our judgment, normally a proper matter for criminal investigation, let alone criminal prosecution'.

Intoxication

This is a defence that students often find difficult to grasp, because the way in which it operates, if at all, depends on variables in terms of the type of intoxication. This could be voluntary or involuntary, and by alcohol, illegal drugs or sedative/prescribed drugs. A further consideration is whether the particular offence charged is an offence of basic or specific intent.

The first general rule is outlined by J. C. Smith and B. Hogan in *Criminal Law* (Butterworths, 7th edn, 1992):

> Intoxication is not and never has been a defence as such, nor is a defect of reason produced by drunkenness...one of the effects of alcohol is to weaken the restraints and inhibitions which normally govern our conduct so a man may do things when drunk that he would never dream of doing while sober. But, if he had the *mens rea* required for the crime, he is guilty even though drink impaired or negatived his ability to judge between right and wrong or to resist provocation, and even though in his drunken state, he found it irresistible to act as he did.

Voluntary intoxication

Alcohol

The legal rule is that intoxication in such cases is at best only a partial defence to offences of specific intent such as murder and s.18 grievous bodily harm with intent. Following the leading case of *DPP* v *Beard*, if the defendant can prove that at the time of committing the crime he or she was so drunk as to be unable to form the necessary *mens rea* of intent for the crime, he or she will be acquitted of that offence but will instead be convicted of the basic intent offence — manslaughter instead of murder, and s.20 instead of s.18 grievous bodily harm. In *DPP* v *Majewski* (1977) this approach was confirmed. The defendant was charged with the assault of a policeman — an offence of basic intent — and his defence of drunkenness was completely rejected.

Illegal drugs

The same position applies to intoxication by illegal drugs. In the leading case of *R* v *Lipman*, the defendant killed his girlfriend, having taken a quantity of LSD and as a result believing that he was being attacked by snakes in the centre of the earth. At his trial, he was acquitted of murder but his plea was not accepted as a defence to manslaughter. The Court of Appeal simply stated that, when the killing results from an unlawful act of the defendant, no specific intent has to be proved to convict the defendant of manslaughter. Self-induced intoxication is no defence and, since the acts complained of were obviously likely to cause harm to the victim, the verdict of manslaughter was inevitable.

Sedative drugs

If the defendant has taken drugs that normally have a sedative or soporific effect, making the user relaxed or sleepy, he or she will usually be treated as involuntarily intoxicated. In *R* v *Hardie* (1984) the defendant took Valium tablets prescribed for the woman with whom he shared a flat and started a fire when she asked him to leave. He was charged and convicted under the **Criminal Damage Act 1971**. However, the Court of Appeal quashed this conviction and overturned the trial judge's direction to the jury, which had made no mention of the distinction in the law between dangerous/illegal and prescription/sedative drugs. The court also indicated that, in this case, the jury should have been invited to consider whether the taking of six Valium tablets by the defendant was objectively reckless.

Involuntary intoxication

This deals with situations in which defendants claim that they did not know that they were taking alcohol or an intoxicating drug, for example in cases where their food or drink has been laced without their knowledge. The legal rule here is that, if this negates the *mens rea* of the offence, it will provide a full defence to any type of offence, whether one of specific or basic intent. However, the outcome of the difficult case of *R* v *Kingston* (1993) seems to contradict this. The defendant was attracted to young boys, and was drugged without his knowledge by his co-defendant, who had intended to blackmail him. His defence to a charge of indecent assault was that the involuntary intoxication effectively disinhibited him, and that, if sober, he would not have carried out these acts. The Court of Appeal allowed his appeal, holding that if a surreptitiously administered drug causes a person to lose his self-control and so form an intent he would not otherwise have formed, the law should not hold him liable as the operative fault is not his. This novel argument was rejected by the House of Lords, which approved the trial judge's direction to the jury. The judge had stated that an intoxicated intent was still intent, and the fact that the intoxication was involuntary made no difference.

Intoxication causing insanity or abnormality of mind

It is settled law that, where excessively heavy drinking causes actual insanity, such as delirium tremens, then the M'Naghten rules apply and the defence becomes one of insanity. It is also clear that self-induced intoxication must be ignored in deciding whether a defendant was suffering from such an abnormality of mind as to amount to diminished responsibility (**Homicide Act 1957**, s.2), unless it can be proved that the craving for drink or drugs was itself an abnormality of mind. You should refer to *R v Dietschmann* (p. 22).

Self-defence/prevention of crime

Where an attack of a violent, unlawful or indecent nature is made, so that the person under attack fears for his or her life or personal safety from injury etc., the person is entitled to protect him or herself and to repel such an attack by force, provided that no more force is used than is reasonable in the circumstances (Lord Morris in *R v Palmer*, 1971).

There is a common law right of self-defence and also a statutory defence in s.3 of the **Criminal Law Act 1967**, which states:

> A person may use such force as is reasonable in the circumstances in the prevention of crime, or in effecting or assisting in the lawful arrest of offenders/suspected offenders or of persons unlawfully at large.

Note that the common law and s.3 can overlap, since the use of reasonable force in self-defence from a murderous assault may also prevent a crime. Where justified, self-defence can provide a complete defence against charges of murder or any non-fatal offence. It negates the unlawfulness of the homicide or assault, in effect rendering the circumstances that surround the act not unlawful.

Defining reasonable force

The factors that may be taken into account in determining what is reasonable force in the context of both common law and statutory defences are:
- the nature and degree of force used
- the gravity of the crime or evil to be prevented
- whether it was possible to prevent the crime by other means
- the relative strengths of the parties concerned and the number of persons involved

The concept of reasonable force, by definition, requires an element of objectivity. In order to reject self-defence/prevention of crime as a defence, the jury must be satisfied that no reasonable person put in the position of the defendant, and with the time for reflection available in the actual case, would consider the violence used by the defendant to be justifiable (*Farrell v Secretary of State for Defence*). But this objectivity must be tempered with the personal situation of the actual defendant. The test is whether the violence used by the defendant was reasonable force in the agony of the situation, and not whether the force used would be considered reasonable by the defendant or a reasonable person viewing the situation in cool isolation.

Further points to consider

- Where defendants have used excessive (and therefore unreasonable) force, neither the common law nor the statutory defence will be open to them, and their criminal liability will be determined by their *mens rea* and the harm they have inflicted.
- The law has no sympathy with persons who are drunk, so an honest mistake made by a drunken defendant will render this defence inadmissible (*R* v *O'Grady*).
- Regarding the duty of the defendant to retreat, in the case of *R* v *Bird* it was held that proof that the defendant had tried to retreat was a method of rebutting the suggestion that the defendant was an attacker, but it was not the only method.
- It appears that in certain circumstances defendants are not obliged to wait until they are attacked before taking steps to protect themselves (*Attorney-General's Reference (No. 2), 1983*).
- Concerning the defence of property, the use of force is not so highly regarded, thus limiting this defence. Professor Ashworth comments in *Principles of Criminal Law* (OUP, 1999):

> What is crucial is that it should rule out the infliction or risk of considerable physical harm merely to apprehend a fleeing thief, to stop minor property loss or damage, etc....The proper approach is to compare the relative value of the rights involved, and not to give special weight to the rights of the property owner simply because the other party is in the wrong (i.e. committing a crime).

Mistake

The issue of mistake can be relevant in two contexts:
- when arguing that the defendant could not have had the *mens rea* required for the crime
- when related to other defences, especially self-defence

Negating *mens rea*

In most cases of mistake, the defendant will argue that the mistake negates the *mens rea* required for that crime. It is established that, in order to be a defence, the mistake must be one of fact and not of law. In *R* v *Reid* a driver refused to be breathalysed because he mistakenly believed that the police officer had no right to require it. The defence was disallowed on the grounds that ignorance of law cannot amount to a mistake.

Self-defence

If the defendant has honestly, but mistakenly, believed him or herself to be under attack etc., he or she must be judged according to this mistaken view of the facts, regardless of whether the mistake was reasonable or not. In the case of *R* v *Williams*, a passerby called Mason saw a youth rob a woman. Mason chased and caught him and knocked him to the ground. Mason then told Williams, who got involved after seeing the youth being attacked by Mason, that he was a police officer (which was untrue) and that he was arresting the youth. Williams asked to see the warrant card and, when this was not produced, a struggle ensued during which Williams punched Mason in the face. In his defence, Williams claimed that he honestly believed that Mason was unlawfully assaulting the youth and that he was trying to rescue the youth. Williams was convicted of actual bodily harm following a direction to the jury that his mistake would be relevant only if it was honest and based on reasonable grounds. On appeal, Lord Lane CJ stated:

> The reasonableness or unreasonableness of the defendant's belief is material to the question of whether the belief was held by the defendant at all. If the belief was in fact held, its unreasonableness, so far as guilt or innocence is concerned, is neither here nor there. It is irrelevant...The jury should be directed first of all that the prosecution have the burden of proving the unlawfulness of the defendant's actions; secondly, if the defendant may have been labouring under a mistake as to the facts, he must be judged according to his mistaken view of the facts, and thirdly, that is so whether the mistake was, on an objective view, a reasonable mistake one or not...Even if the jury come to the conclusion that the mistake was an unreasonable one, if the defendant may genuinely have been labouring under it, he is entitled to rely on it.

The Judicial Studies Board has produced a model direction on self-defence that states the following:

> Whether the plea is self-defence or defence of another, if the defendant may have been labouring under a mistake as to the facts, he must be judged according to his mistaken view of the facts: that is so whether the mistake was, on an objective view, a reasonable mistake or not.

Critical evaluation of fatal and non-fatal offences

The third part of the exam question for this unit assesses how well you can evaluate or criticise a particular area of law. This could be homicide in general, murder or involuntary manslaughter as separate offences, or non-fatal offences. In this section you will find specific textual material on some of these issues which will assist you in dealing with this kind of question.

The major problems that result in weak answers from candidates are as follows:
- **Lack of planning**. All law questions demand a level of planning, and these questions in particular. You must leave ample time for this aspect of the exam; otherwise you will almost certainly make the mistakes described below. Draw

spider diagrams or write some other outline of your answer, in terms of both actual content and structure.
- **Poor time management**. The critical evaluation question comprises a third of the overall marks for the unit, and must therefore receive at least a third of the time allocation.
- **Writing a response that repeats the rules of an issue of law you have already explained or applied in answer to an earlier question**. Some marks will be awarded for this kind of answer, but never high marks, since such answers fail to address the question.
- **Failing to recognise the difference between criticism and evaluation**. Criticism asks the question, 'What is wrong with this area of law?' Evaluation, on the other hand, while requiring a well-explained analysis of weaknesses in the law, also necessitates consideration of the aspects of the law which are broadly satisfactory, followed by a reasoned conclusion.

Although the question does not always ask you specifically to explain what improvements or reforms could be made to the law, marks are awarded to candidates who include such material. Ideally, this should be a summary of Law Commission recommendations, but don't be afraid to include your own ideas as well, especially if these are based on topical debates.

Criticisms of non-fatal offences

Definitions

Non-fatal offences are badly defined. There is still no clear statutory definition of assault and battery, while the definitions of the more serious offences are contained in the Offences Against the Person Act, which was passed over 100 years ago. Professor J. C. Smith described the Act as 'a rag-bag of offences brought together from a wide variety of sources with no attempt, as the draftsman frankly acknowledged, to introduce consistency as to substance or as to form'. Much of the vocabulary is antiquated and even misleading, such as '**assault**' in s.47 assault occasioning actual bodily harm and '**maliciously**' in s.18 wounding or causing grievous bodily harm with intent. In s.18 'maliciously' means nothing in its primary use because the *mens rea* is already defined as 'with intent', whereas in s.20 malicious wounding or inflicting grievous bodily harm means with recklessness or basic intent to inflict some harm. The word '**wounding**' also has a technical rather than the common definition; although the Joint Charging Standard substantially clarifies which charge to bring for different levels of injury, nonetheless any injury that causes blood to flow could potentially be charged as wounding — even a minor cut or a grazed knee.

Another linguistic criticism concerns the use of '**inflict**' in s.20. It is argued that 'inflict' requires a battery to take place for the full offence to be committed. This was the central issue raised in *R* v *Burstow*, which was decided by the House of Lords, where the Court of Appeal dealt with the question of 'Whether an offence of inflicting grievous bodily harm under s.20 can be committed where no physical violence is applied directly or indirectly'. It was argued that it is inherent in the word 'inflict' that there must be a some application of force to the body. However, in the earlier case of *R v Wilson* Lord Roskill was 'content to accept that there can be the infliction of GBH contrary to s.20 without an assault (battery) being committed.'

The use of '**cause**' in s.18 poses further problems. Lord Steyn, in the leading judgment *R v Ireland*, ruled that 'there is no radical difference between the meaning of the words "cause" and "inflict" '. Lord Hope went even further when he stated, 'for all practical purposes there is, in my opinion, no difference between these two words'. In a later section, he continued, 'in the context of a criminal act therefore the words "cause" and "inflict" may be taken to be interchangeable'.

You should be aware of the secondary *mens rea* for an s.18 offence — 'intention to resist or prevent the lawful apprehension of any person'. Although it was stated in *R v Mowatt* that the word 'malicious' means nothing, Professors Smith and Hogan (in *Criminal Law,* Butterworths, 7th edn, 1992) argue that in this particular section the prosecution must prove that the defendant, in seeking to avoid arrest, was at least reckless as to causing some harm. Nevertheless, it is obvious that the respective *mens rea* elements for an s.18 offence are significantly 'unbalanced'.

Hierarchy of seriousness

The hierarchy of the non-fatal offences in terms of seriousness can also be severely criticised. While assault and battery can only be punished with a maximum of 6 months' imprisonment, and s.47 assault occasioning actual bodily harm by 5 years, the only real difference between them is that actual bodily harm is caused, and yet it can mean as little as causing discomfort to the person. In addition, s.20 malicious wounding or inflicting grievous bodily harm is defined as a much more serious offence than s.47 in both *actus reus* and *mens rea*, and yet they share the same maximum sentence. Although it is accepted judicial practice that the maximum sentence will rarely be imposed, and then only for the most severe offence, it remains manifestly unfair that the maximum sentences should be identical when both the *actus reus* and the *mens rea* required for an s.20 conviction are much greater than those for s.47.

A further problem is that arguably the only significant difference between s.20 and s.18 wounding or causing grievous bodily harm with intent is a slightly more serious *mens rea*, yet the maximum sentence leaps from 5 years to life imprisonment. It should be noted that only 23% of offenders indicted under s.18 are eventually convicted of that offence with most of the remainder being convicted of (or having the charge reduced to) lesser offences such as s.20. While there are many reasons for this, one clear factor is the difficulty in proving the required specific intention for s.18. This can perhaps be justified by the fact that a defendant who intends to cause grievous bodily harm within s.18 has the *mens rea* of murder, and it is merely chance that dictates whether the victim of a stabbing survives or dies.

Constructive intent

Possibly the most serious criticism that can be directed against the present law is the issue of constructive intent seen in both s.47 assault occasioning actual bodily harm and s.20 malicious wounding or inflicting grievous bodily harm offences. The defendant is liable to a possible 5-year sentence in terms of the outcome of the offence — which will in many cases have been unforeseen and unintended — rather than in the degree of *mens rea*. This runs counter to the basic requirement of criminal liability, which is that liability should depend on and indeed reflect the amount of fault (i.e. *mens rea*) possessed by the defendant.

Case and statutory law

The final criticism is of the ways in which the statutory offences in the Offences Against the Person Act 1861 are almost constantly redefined through reported cases. It is unsatisfactory for so many changes to be made to statutory offences by means of case law, which by its very nature can be amended through later cases being appealed to the Court of Appeal or to the House of Lords. This is both an unnecessary and expensive appeals process, arising from wrong decisions on questions of law.

The cases of *Ireland* and *Burstow* have considerably extended the law on assault and s.20 grievous bodily harm and, at the time of writing, the case of *R v Mohammed Dica* seems fated to create a further major extension to the definition of grievous bodily harm. In this case, the defendant was convicted of causing 'biological' grievous bodily harm when he tricked two women into having sexual intercourse with him, even though he had been diagnosed with HIV in 1995. This follows the conviction in Scotland of Stephen Kelly in 2001 for 'reckless conduct', after passing HIV to his wife. The Court of Appeal quashed Mohammed Dica's conviction and ordered a retrial to consider the defence's argument of consent. However, the court did rule that injury by reckless infection in the course of sexual activity *does* fall within the scope of s.20, as long as the victim did not consent to run the risk. This ruling overrules the case of *R v Clarence* (1889), where a husband was prosecuted for infecting his unsuspecting wife with gonorrhoea, but his conviction was quashed by a House of Lords ruling that s.20 required an assault or some form of direct bodily violence. In the *New Law Journal* (21 May 2004), J. R. Spencer QC writes that the court condemned *Clarence* as inconsistent with later cases, notably *Ireland* and *Burstow*, which hold that s.20 covers deliberate harassment leading to psychiatric injury: 'If pysychiatric injury can be inflicted without direct or indirect violence or an assault, for the purposes of s.20 physical injury may be similarly inflicted'.

Even more importantly, the Court of Appeal has apparently widened the scope of the defence of consent in such cases, distinguishing the case of *R v Brown*, in which this defence was expressly disallowed by the House of Lords. The court ruled that 'there is a vital difference between consenting to the *deliberate* infliction of harm, and consenting to an activity that you know involves a *risk* of it'. This ruling means that criminal liability does not arise when the other party knows of, or suspects, and is prepared to take, the risk.

Recent developments

The draft Criminal Law Bill issued by the Home Office in 1998 (based on the recommendations of the Law Commission in 1993) updates the language used for non-fatal offences by talking about serious injury rather than grievous bodily harm, and avoiding the words 'maliciously' and 'wounding' altogether. Under the bill, s.18 'wounding or causing grievous bodily harm with intent' is replaced with 'intentionally causing serious injury' (maximum sentence: life imprisonment); s.20 'malicious wounding or inflicting grievous bodily harm' is replaced by 'recklessly causing serious injury' (maximum sentence: 7 years' imprisonment); and s.47 'assault occasioning actual bodily harm' is replaced by 'intentionally or recklessly causing injury' (maximum sentence: 5 years' imprisonment). But the bill continues the term 'assault' for the two separate offences of assault and battery.

Interestingly, the preamble to the Home Office consultation paper 'Violence: Reforming the Offences against the Person Act 1861' reads:

> It is therefore particularly important that the law governing such behaviour should be robust, clear and well understood. Unclear or uncertain criminal law risks creating injustice and unfairness to individuals as well as making the work of the police and courts far more difficult and time-consuming.

Six years after these words were written — and 11 years after the Law Commission published its recommendations — these issues have still not been the subject of legislative reform. Governments have not found the necessary parliamentary time or commitment.

Criticisms of the law of homicide

Murder

Mandatory life sentence

The mandatory life sentence for murder means that the trial judge cannot discriminate between different kinds of murder. Thus the mass murderer Peter Sutcliffe (the 'Yorkshire Ripper') receives the same sentence as the caring relative who, as an act of mercy, kills a spouse dying of a painful terminal illness (see the case of Dr Nigel Cox). Is murder such a unique crime that there cannot be different levels of liability?

The House of Lords Select Committee on Murder and Imprisonment reported in 1988–89 as follows:

> The Committee agree with the majority of their witnesses that the mandatory life sentence for murder should be abolished. Among the considerations which carried most weight with the Committee was the weight of judicial opinion — the Lord Chief Justice and 12 out of 19 judges in the High Court and the Court of Appeal were in favour of a discretionary sentence.

According to D.A. Thomas in *Reshaping the Criminal Law* (ed. Glazebrook, Stevens and Sons, 1978), the usual justification for the life sentence is misdirected:

> The present definition of murder is clearly not a satisfactory basis for selecting offenders for a unique variety of sentencing procedure. In so far as the mandatory life sentence is justified by the special problems of estimating the chances of future violence by those who have killed once, the existence of special defences, such as diminished responsibility and provocation, undermines the logic of the sentence by excepting from its scope just those offenders who are most likely to prove dangerous for the future. If the justification for mandatory life sentence is the unique gravity of the offence and the need to emphasise the particular abhorrence of society for the murderer, that justification is at least diluted by the extension of the definition of murder to include the fortuitous killer.

Partial defences

The legal fiction of 'voluntary manslaughter', which is the only crime with which you can be convicted but not charged, could be dispensed with by removing the mandatory life sentence. This would then enable the pleas of provocation and diminished responsibility to be made to the court in mitigation of sentence.

At the time of writing, the Solicitor-General has directed the Law Commission to review the law on provocation with a view to reforming or even abolishing this defence in the new Domestic Violence Bill. The reason for this referral is the number of men who kill their partners and avoid the mandatory life sentence for murder by successfully pleading provocation. In the view of the Solicitor-General, this plea effectively amounts to 'blaming the victim for her own death'.

Other specific criticisms can also be made of provocation, the most important of which undoubtedly surrounds the 'reasonable man' test, which has undergone major changes in the cases of *R v Morhall* and *R v Smith* (see pp. 24–25).

Intention

Glanville Williams summed up the problem of intention very clearly when he wrote:

> Why is it that intention, or intent, one of the basic concepts of the criminal law, remains so unclear? Judges decline to define it, and they appear to adjust it from one case to another.

Since the case of *DPP v Smith* in 1961, this key element of the law of homicide has undergone considerable changes in the way it is defined, in terms of foreseeability and probability (see the cases of *Moloney*, *Hyams*, *Hancock* and more recently *Nedrick* and *Woollin*).

Because these changes have been case-law led, it is always open to the House of Lords (or even to the Court of Appeal) to vary the definition of intent. As Professor C. M. V. Clarkson writes in his book *Understanding Criminal Liability* (1995, Fontana Press):

> ...these decisions...leave the law in a state of confusion and uncertainty and open the door to inconsistency in jury verdicts...this lack of definition and certainty is highly undesirable and simply invites prejudice, discrimination and abuse.

The present definition of intent — the defendant's foresight of death or grievous bodily harm as virtually certain (as illustrated by both *Nedrick* and *Woollin*) — makes it difficult for the prosecution to obtain a murder conviction. Note the importance of s.8 of the **Criminal Justice Act 1967**:

> A court or jury, in determining whether a person has committed an offence — (a) shall not be bound in law to infer that he intended or foresaw a result of his actions by reasons only of its being a natural and probable consequence of those actions; but (b) shall decide whether he did intend that result by reference to all the evidence, drawing such inferences as appear proper in the circumstances.

This section of the Act effectively ensures that the question of intention is essentially a jury issue, to be decided on the basis of the evidence and therefore not open to judicial definition. Consequently, it must be the strict position that a jury directed along the lines of *Nedrick* and *Woollin* could hold that the defendant did foresee death or serious injury as 'being virtually certain', but that the defendant nonetheless did not intend to kill or commit grievous bodily harm, and is therefore not guilty of murder.

Mens rea

The present *mens rea* of murder, malice aforethought and intent to kill or commit grievous bodily harm, has long been the subject of criticism. The following passages lay out the respective positions.

In 'The mental element in the crime of murder' (*Law Quarterly Review*, 1988), Lord Goff argued:

> I must emphasise that murder is a crime at common law; and that the definition of the mental element is therefore a common law, and not a statutory definition...the mental element in the crime of murder used to be called 'malice aforethought'. This is, of course, thoroughly misleading since neither premeditation nor malice towards the victim were necessary. Furthermore there were three kinds of malice aforethought — express malice, implied malice and constructive malice (the last of these — murder felony — was abolished by s.1 of the Homicide Act 1957).

In the case of *R v Vickers* (1957), Lord Goddard CJ stated:

> If a person does an act which amounts to the infliction of GBH, he cannot say that he only intended to cause a certain degree of harm — he must take the consequences. If he intends to inflict GBH and that person dies, that has always been held in English law sufficient to imply the malice aforethought which is a necessary constituent of murder.

This judgment concerning implied malice was confirmed in *R v Cunningham* (1981), although in a dissenting judgment Lord Edmund-Davies stated:

The view I favour is that there should be no conviction for murder unless an intent to kill is established, the wide range of punishment for manslaughter being fully adequate to deal with all less heinous forms of homicide. I find it passing strange that a person can be convicted of murder if death results from, say, his intentional breaking of another's arm, an action which, while undoubtedly involving the infliction of 'really serious harm' and, as such, calling for severe punishment, would in most cases be unlikely to kill. And yet, for the lesser offence of attempted murder, nothing less than an intention to kill will suffice. But I recognise the force of the contrary view that the outcome of intentionally inflicting serious harm can be so unpredictable that anyone prepared to act so wickedly has little ground for complaint if, where death results, he is convicted and punished as severely as one who intended to kill.

In the case of *Powell* (1999), Lord Steyn said:

[Lord Davies' ruling turns] murder into a constructive crime [resulting] in defendants being classified as murderers who are not in truth murderers...it results in the imposition of mandatory life sentences when neither justice nor the needs of society require the classification of the case as murder.

Andrew Ashworth, in *Principles of Criminal Law* (OUP, 1999), debates the issue as follows:

Does the 'grievous bodily harm' (implied malice) rule extend the definition of murder too far? If the point of distinguishing murder from manslaughter is to mark out the most heinous group of killings for the extra stigma of a murder conviction, it can be argued that this rule draws the line too low. In terms of principle, the rule requires justification because it departs from the principle of correspondence, namely that the fault element in a crime should relate to the consequences prohibited by that crime. By allowing implied malice to suffice for a murder conviction, the law is violating this general principle, effectively turning the most serious offence into a constructive crime. The key argument in favour of this is that death is final and irremediable, unlike even the most serious non-fatal offence. Murder is the gravest crime, and there is no significant moral difference between someone who chooses to cause really serious injury and one who sets out to kill. No one can predict whether a serious injury will result in death — that may depend on the victim's physique, the speed of an ambulance and the quality of medical treatment. If a person chooses to cause serious injury to another, it should be presumed that he/she realises that there is always the risk of death, and such cases show a sufficiently wanton disregard for life as to warrant the label 'murder'. The counter-argument holds that the breach of the principle of correspondence is unnecessary when the amplitude of the crime of manslaughter (and its maximum sentence of life imprisonment) lies below murder. In the leading case of *R v Cunningham*, Lord Edmund-Davies gave the example of breaking someone's arm which constitutes GBH but which is unlikely to endanger the victim's life. If this should result in the victim's death, the attacker would be convicted of murder.

The Criminal Law Revision Committee presented the following arguments in its fourteenth report (1980):

> One of the principal reasons for preserving murder as a separate offence is the stigma that attaches to it and the deterrent effect which that stigma may have. It is important that the definition of murder should, as far as possible, ensure that those convicted of murder will be deserving of the stigma.

> It is wrong in principle that a person should be liable to be convicted of murder who neither intended nor was reckless as to the most important element in the offence, namely death. The consequence of that is that an intention to cause serious bodily harm...should cease to be a sufficient mental element for murder.

Involuntary manslaughter

An important issue is the definition of this offence. It is the only serious offence for which the *mens rea* is defined 'in the negative' — unlawful killing without malice aforethought. It has been said that, whereas murder is defined largely but not exclusively in terms of an intention to kill, manslaughter is defined largely but not exclusively in terms of the absence of such intention.

Within this single offence, there are either two or three different types of involuntary manslaughter, and still no clear consensus as to whether reckless manslaughter exists as a separate head. Lord Mackay LC in *R* v *Adomako* seemed to eliminate reckless manslaughter from the category of involuntary manslaughter, ruling that there was only unlawful and dangerous act manslaughter and gross negligence manslaughter.

Unlawful and dangerous act manslaughter

There are many criticisms of this offence. The first is the issue of constructive liability with reference to the required *mens rea*. If the defendant threatens to throw an object at the victim and the victim, to avoid this, leans back, strikes his or her head and because of a 'thin skull' sustains fatal injuries, the conviction of manslaughter is based on the amount of *mens rea* required for the minor crime of assault. It can be argued that for this offence there need be no correspondence between the defendant's culpability and the resultant death. On the other hand, it has been claimed that since manslaughter is largely a crime of violence, there is relevant culpability because the defendant has chosen to engage in a violent attack on the victim.

This view would be stronger if the requirement of an 'unlawful and dangerous act' was defined much more narrowly in terms of a crime of violence and dangerousness, in the sense that there was subjective recklessness as to causing serious harm. Following *R* v *G*, it can also be argued strongly that the objective requirement of the test of dangerousness should be rejected. It must surely be absurd that, unless the Crown succeeds in proving the defendant knew of the risk he or she was running, he or she can be acquitted of criminal damage inflicted recklessly but can nonetheless be convicted of the much more serious crime of manslaughter on the grounds of objective dangerousness.

Another criticism is that the present law on unlawful acts does not require the act to be a violent act against a person. This has led to considerable confusion in the context of supplying and/or injecting unlawful drugs, as the contrasting cases of *Dalby* and *Cato* illustrate.

Gross negligence manslaughter
Definition
The first criticism is that the definition of this serious criminal offence is actually based largely on civil law rules — the tort of negligence — which is employed to determine whether a duty of care was owed by the defendant to the victim and whether that duty was breached. The comparison with unlawful act manslaughter with regard to this test could not be more unfair: how can a defendant be convicted of one type of involuntary manslaughter on the basis of a tort when a criminal act is required as the basis of the other type?

It is essentially the responsibility of the jury to determine gross negligence. The test established in *R* v *Bateman* requires the jury to decide whether the defendant's conduct was 'so bad' as to justify a conviction for manslaughter. This approach is circular in that the members of the jury are invited to convict the defendant of a crime if they think the defendant's conduct was unlawful.

Professor Clarkson also criticises this offence on the basis 'that criminal liability and punishment should be linked to moral guilt which can be perceived as blaming only those who have chosen to cause harm, either through intention or recklessness'. For such a serious offence, the test of recklessness would have to be the subjective Cunningham test, which has been adopted for non-fatal offences such as s.47 actual bodily harm and s.20 malicious wounding or inflicting grievous bodily harm. But because gross negligence is based on civil law negligence, the test is the objective one of 'the reasonable man'.

A final argument against the present definition of this offence is that there appears to be no rule as to the level of risk that needs to be involved for gross negligence to arise. In *Adomako*, the House of Lords declined to define how serious the risk should be, whether in terms of injury, serious injury or death. The test in *R* v *Stone and Dobinson* was that of risk to health. Since that case, the Court of Appeal significantly narrowed this test in *R* v *Singh*. The trial judge ruled that 'the circumstances must be such that a reasonably prudent person would have foreseen a serious and obvious risk not merely of injury, even serious injury, but of death'. Without a statutory definition, this test is of course subject to judicial change at any time.

Mens rea
Glanville Williams, a leading law academic, argues that neither negligence, even if gross, nor objective recklessness is a sufficient *mens rea* base for a crime as serious as involuntary manslaughter. He feels that the appropriate *mens rea* should be intention to cause serious harm, or subjective recklessness as to whether death or serious personal injury will be caused. In the *New Law Journal* (8 October 1993) he states:

> ...a fault basis of liability should focus on the degree of fault of the offender rather than on the extent of mischief he has caused; a restriction of manslaughter to cases of gross negligence is insufficient. Putting manslaughter on a basis of subjective recklessness would protect inadequate people from inappropriate charges of this gravity. It would leave other provision to be made for cases where it is thought necessary to punish acts of gross but unthinking negligence causing death or injury, but they should be offences of a lower order than manslaughter.

He also comments that the requirement 'risk of injury to health' is too vague a phrase, and states that the fault element should be as to the risk of causing death or serious injury. Even a requirement that negligence must be gross is inadequate to impose proper limits on the law of manslaughter. By hypothesis, a death has been caused and it is consequently easy for prosecutor, judge and jury to conclude that, since the event was terrible in terms of the fatal consequence, the negligence must have been gross.

Even the name 'manslaughter' is inept; the doctors in *R* v *Prentice* did not 'slaughter' their patient — they neither intended to kill him nor were subjectively reckless as to this fact. Glanville Williams considers that:

> ...manslaughter should require a mental element because it is a wide-ranging crime with a fearsome maximum punishment. Moreover the mental element is of such critical importance for sentencing that the jury should be enabled to pronounce upon it.

Suggested reforms

To reform this generally unsatisfactory area of law, the Law Commission in its Draft Code (Clause 55) recommended that both unlawful and dangerous act manslaughter and gross negligence manslaughter should be abolished and replaced by the following offences:

(1) *Reckless killing*, which would be committed if:
   (a) a person by his or her conduct caused the death of another, and he or she is aware of a risk that the conduct will cause death or serious injury; and
   (b) it is unreasonable for him or her to take that risk. Recklessness is restricted to its subjective meaning.

The maximum proposed sentence for reckless killing would be life imprisonment.

(2) *Killing by gross negligence*, which requires:
   (a) that a person by his or her conduct causes the death of another; and
   (b) a risk that that conduct will cause death or serious injury would be obvious to a reasonable person; and
   (c) he or she is capable of appreciating that risk; and either
   (d) his or her conduct falls far below what can reasonably be expected in the circumstances, or
   (e) he or she intends by that conduct to cause some injury, or is aware of, and unreasonably takes, the risk that it may do so and the conduct causing the injury constitutes an offence.

The maximum proposed sentence for killing by gross negligence would be 10 years' imprisonment.

Questions & Answers

This section of the guide provides you with seven questions which cover most of the Unit 4 topics, both offences and defences. Each question is followed by an A-grade answer which demonstrates both the structure that you should follow and how to use case and statutory authorities. Question 3 has three parts, which is the format used in the exam.

C-grade answers have also been included with questions 3 and 7 to illustrate some of the common problems that unnecessarily lead to students achieving lower marks. Note the importance of using cases effectively — failure to use cases is one of the most significant differences between A- and C-grade answers.

To acquire the necessary skills and become more familiar with this style of examination question, it is a good idea to practise adapting the A-grade answers for different scenarios. You are strongly encouraged to download past papers and mark schemes from AQA (www.aqa.org.uk) or to obtain these from your teacher.

The mnemonic **IDEA** may help you answer 'problem-solving' questions based on a short scenario:
- **I** **Identify** both the appropriate offence(s) and defence(s).
- **D** **Define** the offence(s) and defence(s).
- **E** **Explain** the various legal rules.
- **A** **Apply** these rules to the facts of the question, using authorities — both cases and statutes — to support your answer.

Examiner's comments

The candidate answers are accompanied by examiner's comments, preceded by the icon 🖉. These explain the elements of the answer for which marks can be awarded, and are intended to give you an insight into what examiners are looking for. For A-grade answers, these comments show why high marks would be given. The comments given for C-grade answers point out the various weaknesses — lack of cases, inadequate explanation and irrelevant material, all of which cause marks to be lost.

Note: the questions on pages 59, 68 and 71 are reproduced by permission of AQA (AEB). Please note that the questions on pages 68 and 71 are *not* from the live examinations for the current specification. For GCE Advanced Level subjects, new specifications were introduced in 2001.

Question 1

Non-fatal offences (I)

Darren and Michael are captains of opposing rugby teams with a history of 'bad blood' between them. These teams are drawn against each other in the semi-final of the regional rugby competition. During this match, Darren tackles Michael as he is about to score a try in injury time. However, the tackle is judged by the referee to be a high one and Darren is sent off the field. As a result of the tackle, Michael's collar bone is fractured and, in falling heavily to the ground, he also loses a tooth.

Discuss Darren's criminal liability for the injuries to Michael. (25 marks)

■ ■ ■

A-grade answer

Given the nature of the injuries which Michael sustained, Darren could be charged with s.20 grievous bodily harm (GBH), s.20 wounding and s.47 assault occasioning actual bodily harm (ABH) — all offences within the Offences against the Person Act 1861. The Joint Charging Standard agreed by the police and the Crown Prosecution Service states that broken bones constitute serious injury, which in *R* v *Saunders* was used to define GBH. The loss of the tooth would normally be charged as a s.47 offence, but as bleeding would have been caused, this could equally be charged as wounding under s.20. Wounding was defined in the case of *C (a minor)* v *Eisenhower* as a breach in both the inner and outer layers of skin.

For both wounding and infliction of GBH under s.20, the *mens rea* is now accepted as being intention or recklessness as to causing some harm, albeit not serious harm. This was established in the case of *R* v *Mowatt*, and confirmed in the later case of *R* v *Grimshaw*. It is therefore not necessary for the prosecution to seek to prove that the defendant intended or was reckless as to causing either GBH or wounding.

> 🖉 The candidate has immediately used the Joint Charging Standard to identify the correct offences and then used relevant cases to define the *actus reus* and *mens rea*. The broken collar bone would certainly be regarded as grievous bodily harm, and the candidate correctly identifies that the loss of a tooth could be treated as wounding within the same s.20.

There can be no doubt that Darren directly caused Michael's injuries — both 'but for' factual causation and legal rules of causation are clearly satisfied, and it could be strongly argued that the high tackle was at least reckless in the Cunningham sense of 'conscious unjustified risk-taking'.

If Darren was to be charged with s.47 assault occasioning ABH for the loss of the tooth, the prosecution would only have to prove that Darren assaulted/battered Michael (inflicting unlawful personal violence) which evidently he did, and did so with the *mens rea* of battery, which is intent or subjective recklessness as to the *actus reus* of battery. There is no need for the prosecution to establish that the defendant intended or was reckless as to causing ABH — this important rule was laid down by the House of Lords in the two cases of *R* v *Savage* and *R* v *Parmenter*, and was re-affirmed in *R* v *Roberts*. In the rugby match, the high tackle on Michael by Darren could certainly be described as reckless.

> It is quite correct to deal with the lost tooth under s.20 wounding, but the candidate would gain additional marks for explaining why the loss of a tooth would be charged under s.47 actual bodily harm. Again, both the *actus reus* and *mens rea* elements are correctly described, with supporting cases.

As to defences which Darren could plead, there would appear to be only one — that of consent. This is a very limited defence and is usually only available in respect of the minor crimes of assault and battery. For the more serious non-fatal offences — ABH and GBH — it can only be successfully pleaded if the activity out of which the injury arises comes under any of the following headings: surgery, including tattooing and body piercing; rough horseplay; sporting activities.

It is this last category with which we are concerned here. The general rule in contact sports such as rugby is that players are presumed to have consented to serious injuries provided these occurred within the rules of the game. For example, this defence was allowed in the case of *R* v *Billinghurst*, which involved a rugby match. In the case presented here, however, it is clear from the referee's decision in sending Darren off the field that the tackle constituted foul play.

> Note how fully the defence of consent is described here — one of the most common weaknesses in this kind of answer is the omission of any defence material or only giving it a passing mention. This question is comprehensively and accurately answered and makes sound use of relevant cases. The candidate would be awarded high marks in the 21–25-mark band.

Non-fatal offences (II)

Critically analyse the present law on non-fatal offences. (25 marks)

■ ■ ■

A-grade answer

The first observation that can be made about non-fatal offences is that they are not completely codified. The separate offences of assault and battery remain common law offences, although their separate nature was confirmed in the Criminal Justice Act 1988, s.39. But the more serious offences — assault occasioning actual bodily harm (ABH), wounding and inflicting grievous bodily harm (GBH), and causing GBH with intent — are contained in the Offences Against the Person Act 1861.

The 1861 Act, even at the time of its passing into law, was rightly described as 'a rag-bag of offences' by its own draftsman, and as it is now over 140 years old, the criticisms are even more acute. The language used to describe the various sections is now archaic: grievous bodily harm, which simply means serious harm; and assault occasioning actual bodily harm, which most commonly means some kind of battery that causes real harm to a victim. The definition given to 'wounding' in *C (a minor)* v *Eisenhower* is far too wide — any breach in the outer and inner layers of the skin. This could cover any minor cut or even a graze. An interesting comparison can be made here with regard to the Theft Act 1968, which was intended to codify the entire law of theft. Within 10 years a further Theft Act had to be passed, and there have been further significant statutory additions and amendments since then; yet the 1861 Act remains unamended (except by judicial interventions).

Other linguistic criticisms concern the words 'assault' and 'battery'. Although technically used to describe 'causing a victim to fear the use of unlawful personal violence', 'assault' is most commonly understood to refer to some sort of physical attack; 'battery' is strictly defined as 'unlawful touching' and no injury of any sort is required.

Probably the most serious attack on the 1861 Act concerns the issue of *mens rea* for each of the offences it describes. In s.47 assault occasioning ABH the statute is entirely silent on the issue of *mens rea* and it has been left to judges to determine what that is. The cases of *R* v *Savage* and *R* v *Parmenter* now confirm that the *mens rea* of assault or battery — intention or subjective recklessness — is all that is required. In s.20 the word 'malicious' has been interpreted to mean 'intention or recklessness as to causing some harm' (*R* v *Mowatt* and *R* v *Grimshaw*). In the most serious section — s.18 — judges and academic lawyers have concluded that the same word is effectively redundant, except in the secondary *mens rea*, intent to resist arrest.

A further obvious point of criticism is that this Act is now undergoing almost perpetual revision and rewriting by judges. This could almost be referred to as 'law-making by statutory interpretation'. The 2003 case of *R v Mohammed Dica*, which involved the conviction of the defendant for s.20 'biological' GBH after infecting two women with the HIV/AIDS virus, is another good example of the ability of senior courts to amend the law. The Court of Appeal, having quashed the conviction and ordered a retrial, confirmed that injury by reckless infection *does* constitute a s.20 offence. The most significant aspect of this judgment is in regard to the defence of consent, as the court ruled that if the other party knew or suspected that his or her partner was infected, no criminal liability would arise.

Given the judicial decisions in *R v Savage* (s.47) and *R v Mowatt* (s.20), it is clear that these two offences now involve constructive liability — for neither offence does the Crown have to prove intention or recklessness as to the *actus reus* of the offence. A conviction for s.47 can be obtained by proving that ABH was in fact caused by common assault and that the defendant either intended or was reckless as to the assault or battery. In neither of these offences is there any need to prove that the defendant intended or was reckless as to causing any level of harm at all. This issue of constructive liability militates against the basic principle of criminal liability, known as the principle of correspondence: that the fault element (*mens rea*) should be related to the *actus reus* of the offence and to the possible consequences of being convicted of that offence.

Finally, the 'hierarchy of sentencing' can be easily criticised. Both assault and battery have the same maximum sentence of 6 months. Section 47 ABH (which need only involve 'any hurt or injury which interferes with the health or comfort of the victim') has a far greater maximum sentence of 5 years. This is exactly the same as for s.20 wounding and inflicting GBH. These maximum sentences lack even a semblance of consistency or coherence.

It is now evident that there is an unarguable case for complete codification of all non-fatal offences, but even the 1994 Law Commission recommendations for reform did not include the common law offences of assault and battery. Furthermore, although these recommendations have been accepted by all subsequent governments, no action has been taken to incorporate them in any of the major Criminal Justice Acts passed since then.

> This answer is both comprehensive and well argued. All the major issues are addressed: the archaic and confusing language; the much-criticised issue of constructive liability; the inconsistency of sentencing levels and the delay in implementing law reform. The candidate uses key cases effectively to illustrate the various points of criticism, and the references to the topical and important case of *R v Dica* is particularly useful. This answer would be awarded the full 25 marks.

Question 3

Grievous bodily harm and involuntary manslaughter

Adrian and Brian were in a nightclub, where Adrian took some drugs. Shortly afterwards, Adrian began to act in a strange manner, giggling and stumbling about. When Adrian clumsily spilled a drink over Chris, Brian decided it was time to get him home. As they left the nightclub, they were followed by Chris and his friend, Don. Chris challenged Adrian to a fight and Adrian took off his jacket and then immediately lashed out at Chris before Chris was prepared. The blow sent him reeling backwards and he dislocated his knee in a very awkward fall.

Meanwhile, Brian had run off but had been caught by Don in a disused building. Don was holding Brian tightly round the neck and causing him to choke, but Brian managed to elbow him twice in the face. Don released his grip, suddenly collapsed, and was sick as he lay on his back. Brian looked at him for a few seconds and then walked away. Don was later found to have died by choking on his vomit.

Source: June 2002, Law Unit 4, question 1.

(a) Discuss Adrian's criminal liability in connection with the injury to Chris. (25 marks)
(b) Discuss Brian's criminal liability for the involuntary manslaughter of Don. (25 marks)
(c) Discuss how satisfactory the present law on involuntary manslaughter is. (25 marks)

■ ■ ■

A-grade answer

(a) In terms of the severity of the injury which Chris sustained — the dislocated knee — Adrian could face a charge under s.20 or s.18 of the Offences Against the Person Act 1861. The Joint Charging Standard agreed between the police and Crown Prosecution Service confirms that a dislocated joint should be charged as grievous bodily harm (GBH).

Section 20 requires that the defendant caused GBH to the victim as the *actus reus* of this offence. Grievous bodily harm was defined as 'really serious harm' in *DPP* v *Smith*, but this was revised to 'serious harm' in *R* v *Saunders*. As the scenario states that 'Adrian lashed out at Chris' and 'the blow sent him reeling', there would appear to be no difficulty in proving the necessary causation — under both the 'but for' and the legal rules of causation. There was no intervening act between the blow and the injury, and Adrian's action was certainly a 'significant contribution' to the dislocated knee as set out in *R* v *Cheshire*.

The *mens rea* of s.20 is now settled as either intention or recklessness to cause some harm. This was decided in *R* v *Mowatt* and confirmed in the later case of

R v *Grimshaw*. It is not therefore necessary for the Crown to prove that the defendant intended to cause GBH or was reckless as to whether this would be the outcome. Here, the circumstances clearly suggest that in starting the fight 'by lashing out at Chris before he was prepared', Adrian intended to cause at least some harm to Chris.

The *actus reus* of s.18 is identical to that of s.20 — either wounding or GBH. The main difference between these two offences is that of *mens rea*. Section 18 is defined as an offence of specific intent. To secure a conviction, the Crown must prove that the defendant intended to cause GBH. Intention can be direct, where the defendant had the aim or purpose of causing GBH, or oblique, where the members of the jury can find the necessary intent if they decide that the defendant foresaw the outcome of GBH as 'virtually certain', as in the cases of *Nedrick* and *Woollin*. However, in the circumstances of the case, the defendant could argue that he or she did not wish the actual outcome.

It would certainly be possible for Adrian to be convicted of a s.18 offence as the action of striking another person so hard that he or she reels backward and falls could be viewed by the jury as falling within the test laid down by these two cases. In a case such as this where no weapon has been used, it is more usual for the Crown to prosecute on the basis of a s.20 charge.

The possible defences open to Adrian are limited. It is a clear rule of law that consent cannot be pleaded to ordinary fighting (*R* v *Donovan*) and certainly not to an incident which has resulted in GBH. If s.20 were to be charged, the defence of intoxication is also unavailable to Adrian, as the cases of *Majewski* and *Lipman* confirm that voluntary intoxication by drink or drugs can only be pleaded as a partial defence to crimes of specific intent. Section 20 is a basic intent crime.

The only other defence would be one of automatism, which if successful negates the *actus reus* of an offence. This requires the defendant to prove that at the material time of the commission of the offence, he or she was not in control of his or her actions. However, here again Adrian would face legal difficulties, because for clear policy reasons the courts are unwilling to allow such a defence if the loss of control has been caused by voluntary intoxication by alcohol or illegal drugs. It is also, of course, quite clear that Adrian was in control of his actions when he attacked Chris.

This is an accurate and well-argued answer in which the candidate uses the Joint Charging Standard to identify the appropriate offence. Both *actus reus* and *mens rea* elements are described clearly with supporting cases. The issue of a possible s.18 charge is explored fully, but in the circumstances of the scenario the candidate has decided correctly against this. In this question there is an obvious problem with the possible defences — none of these would actually be successful. Students often make errors when writing about intoxication, but this candidate deals with the issue decisively, using the correct cases. This is also true of his or her discussion of both consent and automatism. This answer would receive 24–25 marks, a high grade A.

(b) Involuntary manslaughter is defined as unlawful killing without malice aforethought, which is intent to kill or commit GBH. It can be committed in two different ways — by unlawful and dangerous act, or by gross negligence. The former requires a positive act, which in this case would be the blows Brian struck with his elbow; gross negligence is committed by an omission, which would be Brian's walking away from Don, who was clearly distressed.

Unlawful and dangerous act manslaughter, also referred to as constructive or Church doctrine manslaughter, first of all requires that the defendant has committed a crime — the unlawful act cannot be a tort or contract (*R* v *Franklin*). By striking Don with his elbows and causing him to collapse, it can be argued that Brian could have committed GBH, and certainly ABH. The *mens rea* for manslaughter is the *mens rea* of the unlawful act; if the charge was s.47 ABH or s.20 GBH, the *mens rea* would be either intention or Cunningham recklessness (conscious taking of an unjustified risk). As the blows by Brian must have been struck with the intent of causing at least some harm to Don, the *mens rea* requirement of both offences s.47 and s.20 is satisfied, and accordingly Brian has the necessary *mens rea* for manslaughter.

The second requirement is that the unlawful act must also be dangerous (*R* v *Church*, confirmed by *DPP* v *Newbury and Jones* as 'dangerous in the sense that a sober and reasonable person would recognise that the act carried the risk of some harm albeit not serious injury'). The use of an elbow to strike the victim twice in the face would certainly satisfy this limited test.

The final test is that the unlawful act must have caused the death of the victim (*R* v *Goodfellow*). Here Brian's attack satisfies both the factual 'but for' test of causation and the legal rules established in *R* v *Smith* and *R* v *Cheshire*. His attack was both the substantial and operating cause of death and a significant contribution to Don's death.

It can therefore be strongly argued that Brian has both the *actus reus* and *mens rea* of unlawful and dangerous act manslaughter.

In respect of his omission in walking away from Don, who was clearly seriously ill, having collapsed and been sick, Brian could be liable for manslaughter by gross negligence. This is based on the civil tort of negligence and requires that there be a duty of care, the breach of which causes the victim's death, and gross negligence which the jury believes makes the act criminal and thus deserving of punishment. The issue of duty of care relies on the incremental tests established in *Caparo* v *Dickman* — foreseeability of harm, proximity and the policy test of whether it is fair, just and reasonable to impose a duty of care. Here, it could be argued that, having struck Don and caused his collapse, the 'reasonable man' would foresee some further harm, and there is clearly proximity in terms of time and space. There is also no policy reason why a duty should not be imposed. It could also be alleged that by walking away in these circumstances, Brian breached his duty of care — this test is also objective and based on 'the reasonable man' test. The issue of causation has already been addressed above.

The final issue, that of gross negligence itself, is one for the jury to decide upon. In the leading case of *R* v *Adomako*, Lord Mackay declined to define what gross negligence meant, choosing to leave this to the jury as he felt that such a definition would be incomprehensible. However, in *R* v *Singh*, the trial judge laid down the following test for the jury: 'The question posed is having regard to the risk of death involved, was the defendant's conduct so bad in all the circumstances as to amount in your judgment to a criminal act or omission?' This direction was later approved by the Court of Appeal. Lord Taylor CJ in *Adomako* had suggested that 'inattention or failure to address a serious risk which goes beyond mere carelessness in respect of an obvious matter which the defendant's duty demanded he should address' could properly lead a jury to make a finding of gross negligence.

In the light of these legal rulings, Brian could be convicted of gross negligence manslaughter, but it remains much more likely on the facts of this case that he would be convicted of unlawful and dangerous act manslaughter.

In his defence, Brian could plead self-defence. It is the position under both common law and statute — Criminal Law Act 1967, s.3 — that a person if attacked is entitled to protect him or herself by using such force as is reasonable in all the circumstances. Where justified this can provide a complete defence by negating the unlawfulness of the homicide or assault — in effect, this defence renders the circumstances which surround the act not unlawful. Given that Don 'was holding Brian tightly round the neck and causing him to choke', it could be argued that Brian's reaction of elbowing him twice in the face was both a proportionate and reasonable use of force. However, while his defence could be successful in terms of the unlawful and dangerous act manslaughter charge, it would not be available against the charge of gross negligence manslaughter.

> This answer immediately and correctly defines the offence of involuntary manslaughter and then identifies the two types — unlawful dangerous act, and gross negligence. The candidate deals with unlawful act first since the facts more obviously suggest this approach, and this form of manslaughter tends to be easier to write about than gross negligence. Note the detailed description of all three rules — unlawful act, dangerousness and causation — with excellent use of supporting cases. The candidate then applies the facts to each rule soundly. The gross negligence answer is fuller than it needs to be given the nature of the scenario and the strong section on unlawful dangerous act manslaughter. The self-defence paragraph is written clearly and refers to both common law and statutory defences. This answer would receive 25 marks.
>
> A good exercise to help you write concisely but comprehensively would be to reduce the overall length of this answer by 20–25% yet still obtain an A grade.

(c) The first issue to address when considering the extent to which the present law of involuntary manslaughter is satisfactory is what the overriding purpose of homicide laws should be. Every jurisdiction recognises that unlawful killing can be committed with different levels of fault liability (*mens rea*), and as a consequence there need to be different categories of offence which reflect these different fault levels. Such offences should be defined clearly and the maximum punishments for each should again reflect the issue of greater or lesser fault.

In England, there are three main categories of homicide — murder, voluntary manslaughter (effectively murder with a partial defence of provocation or diminished responsibility) and involuntary manslaughter. Murder carries a mandatory life sentence, while both categories of manslaughter carry a maximum but discretionary life sentence — this fact alone confirms that there is a problem with manslaughter. In other jurisdictions, there is greater differentiation between homicide offences and this is reflected in lower levels of maximum penalty.

The first important issue is the definition of the offence of involuntary manslaughter. It is the only serious offence for which the *mens rea* is defined 'in the negative' — unlawful killing without malice aforethought.

An additional problem arises when one considers that, within this single offence, there are either two or three different types of involuntary manslaughter, and still no clear consensus as to whether reckless manslaughter exists as a separate head. Lord Mackay LC in *R* v *Adomako* seemed to eliminate reckless manslaughter from the category of involuntary manslaughter, ruling that there was only unlawful and dangerous act manslaughter and gross negligence manslaughter.

There are many criticisms of unlawful and dangerous act manslaughter. The first is the issue of constructive liability with reference to the required *mens rea*. If the defendant threatens to throw an object at the victim and the victim, to avoid this, leans back, strikes his or her head and because of a 'thin skull' sustains fatal injuries, the conviction of manslaughter is based on the amount of *mens rea* required for the minor crime of assault. It can be argued that for this offence there need be no correspondence between the defendant's culpability and the resultant death. On the other hand, it has been claimed that since manslaughter is largely a crime of violence, there is relevant culpability because the defendant has chosen to engage in a violent attack on the victim. This view would be stronger if the requirement of an 'unlawful and dangerous act' was defined much more narrowly in terms of a crime of violence and dangerousness, in the sense that there was subjective recklessness.

Another criticism is that the present law on unlawful act does not require the act to be a violent act against a person. This has led to considerable confusion within the context of supplying and/or injecting unlawful drugs, as the contrasting cases of *Dalby* and *Cato* illustrate.

The second head of involuntary manslaughter is that of gross negligence and again there are many criticisms that can be directed against this offence. The first is that this serious criminal offence is actually based largely on civil law rules — the tort of negligence — which are employed to determine whether a duty of care was owed by the defendant to the victim and whether that duty was breached. The test established in *R* v *Bateman* requires the jury to decide whether the defendant's conduct was 'so bad' as to justify a conviction for manslaughter. This approach is circular in that the members of the jury are invited to convict the defendant of a crime if they think the defendant's conduct was unlawful.

Professor Clarkson also criticises this offence on the basis that 'criminal liability and punishment should be linked to moral guilt which can be perceived as blaming only those who have chosen to cause harm, either through intention or recklessness'. For such a serious offence, the test of recklessness would have to be the subjective Cunningham test, which has been adopted for non-fatal offences such as s.47 actual bodily harm or s.20 malicious wounding or inflicting grievous bodily harm.

A final argument against the present definition of this offence is that there appears to be no rule as to the level of risk that needs to be involved for gross negligence to arise. In *Adomako*, the House of Lords declined to define how serious the risk should be, whether in terms of injury, serious injury or death. The test in R v *Stone and Dobinson* was that of risk to health. The Court of Appeal significantly narrowed this test in R v *Singh*. The trial judge ruled that 'the circumstances must be such that a reasonably prudent person would have foreseen a serious and obvious risk not merely of injury, even serious injury, but of death'. Without a statutory definition, this test is of course subject to judicial change at any time.

Glanville Williams, a leading law academic, argues that neither negligence, even if gross, nor objective recklessness is a sufficient *mens rea* base for a crime as serious as involuntary manslaughter. He feels that the appropriate *mens rea* should be intention to cause serious harm, or subjective recklessness as to whether death or serious personal injury will be caused. He states that 'a fault basis of liability should focus on the degree of fault of the offender rather than on the extent of mischief he has caused; a restriction of this offence to cases of gross negligence is insufficient. Putting manslaughter on a basis of subjective recklessness would protect inadequate people from inappropriate charges of this gravity. It would leave other provision to be made for cases where it is thought necessary to punish acts of gross but unthinking negligence causing death or injury, but they should be offences of a lower order than manslaughter'.

To reform this generally unsatisfactory area of law, the Law Commission in its Draft Code (Clause 55) recommended that both unlawful and dangerous act manslaughter and gross negligence manslaughter should be abolished and replaced by the following offences:

(1) Reckless killing, which would be committed if:
  (a) a person by his or her conduct caused the death of another, and he or she is aware of a risk that the conduct will cause death or serious injury; and
  (b) it is unreasonable for him or her to take that risk. Recklessness is restricted to its subjective meaning.

(2) Killing by gross negligence, which requires:
  (a) that a person by his or her conduct causes the death of another; and
  (b) a risk that that conduct will cause death or serious injury would be obvious to a reasonable person; and
  (c) he or she is capable of appreciating that risk; and either

(d) his or her conduct falls far below what can reasonably be expected in the circumstances, or

(e) he or she intends by that conduct to cause some injury, or is aware of, and unreasonably takes, the risk that it may do so and the conduct causing the injury constitutes an offence.

🖉 This is much longer than is necessary for an A-grade answer to this question. The final section on the Law Commission reform recommendations is certainly not required, but if time permits, such a section, even in summary form, will always attract additional marks. The answer is well structured, with a strong introductory paragraph followed by a detailed analysis of both heads of involuntary manslaughter. The inclusion of case authorities makes the criticism much more convincing, as does the citation of arguments advanced by leading academic lawyers such as Professors Clarkson and Glanville Williams. The answer would receive the full 25 marks.

As suggested in part (b), summarising this long answer by reducing it by 20–25% yet still retaining an A-grade answer would be a useful exercise in writing concisely.

■ ■ ■

C-grade answer

(a) Adrian could possibly be liable for a s.20 offence under the Offences Against the Person Act 1861. The *actus reus* of this is to inflict grievous bodily harm (GBH) or wounding, but it is unlikely to be wounding as there is no evidence of bleeding. The dislocated knee could be charged as GBH, following *R* v *Saunders*. There is no problem with the issue of causing this injury as Adrian punched Chris and this blow caused him to fall. The *mens rea* of s.20 is that of Cunningham subjective recklessness — it seems clear that Adrian did not intend to cause a serious injury but he certainly was reckless. The leading case here is *R* v *Mowatt*.

Another possible offence which Adrian may be guilty of is that of s.47 actual bodily harm (ABH). The *actus reus* is causing ABH and the *mens rea* is the same as that for assault or battery — this was confirmed by the cases of *Savage* and *Parmenter*. As Adrian deliberately hit Chris, which would be enough for battery, he has the required level of *mens rea* for s.47.

🖉 Contrast this attempt with the A-grade answer above. This candidate makes no reference to the Joint Charging Standard and both s.20 and s.47 offences are explained much more cursorily. A particular and common weakness is the failure to explain that the *mens rea* for s.20 is either intention or recklessness as to causing some harm.

In his defence, Adrian may try to rely on consent, particularly since it was Chris who first challenged Adrian to fight. However, this defence is rarely successful if a serious injury has occurred in a fight. The issue of intoxication is also likely to prove unhelpful, since the fact that Adrian had voluntarily taken drugs probably weakens this defence. A good case to illustrate this problem is *R* v *Lipman* where the defendant took LSD and hallucinated that he was at the centre of the earth being attacked by a giant snake, which he then attacked. He had in fact killed his girlfriend. His defence of intoxication was rejected by the court.

> In common with many such answers, the candidate's analysis of the defences is unconvincing. No cases are cited to support the discussion of consent and there is no reference to the exception of sporting injuries. Also omitted from the defence of intoxication is the important issue of basic and specific intention offences. This answer would receive 13 or 14 marks.

(b) As there is no evidence of intention on the part of Brian either to kill or to inflict GBH, this cannot be murder.

> This comment is irrelevant since the actual question states that the offence is involuntary manslaughter.

The offence of involuntary manslaughter can be committed either by an unlawful and dangerous act or by gross negligence. The facts of the scenario mean that Brian could be liable under both types. For unlawful and dangerous act manslaughter, the defendant must have carried out a crime — in this case the elbowing of Don in the face would be enough — and also the act must be dangerous (*R* v *Church*), which is an objective test. The final requirement is that the act caused the death of the victim, which is the case here since there is no intervening act.

> The difference between this answer and the A-grade answer could not be clearer. This candidate does not provide a definition for involuntary manslaughter, and the explanation is superficial, with no specific reference made to the *mens rea* requirement.

Having given Don the injuries which caused him to collapse, Brian walked away without trying to help him or to summon an ambulance. It seems possible for Brian to be guilty of gross negligence manslaughter which was laid down in the case of *R* v *Adomako*. This offence requires the prosecution to prove that the defendant owed the victim a duty of care, that the defendant then breached that duty and the breach caused the victim's death, and the defendant's negligence was so serious as to constitute a crime in the minds of the jurors. Here it seems clear that Brian did owe Don a duty, having inflicted such injuries that Don collapsed, and that by walking away he then breached that duty, which caused Don's death by choking on his vomit. The issue of gross negligence is for the jury to decide.

> Again, the candidate makes no attempt to explain the duty of care requirement or indeed any of the key issues of this offence.

Brian could plead self-defence because Don had caught Brian and held him round the neck, causing him to choke. This defence requires the defendant to have used reasonable force and Brian elbowing Don twice could be described as reasonable force. However, it is not clear if this defence would work for the crime of gross negligence although it would for unlawful act manslaughter.

> 🖉 This is a weak account of self-defence with no reference to the Criminal Law Act. Overall, the answer is unconvincing, both in terms of legal explanations and application. Although the candidate correctly identifies the key components required for the question set, there is no depth to his or her explanation. The case references are also poor, particularly with regard to unlawful act manslaughter. This answer would receive 13 marks — a mid grade C.

(c) Involuntary manslaughter consists of two different types — unlawful and dangerous act manslaughter and gross negligence manslaughter — although some authorities still argue that there is a further type, that of reckless manslaughter.

The first criticism concerning gross negligence manslaughter is that negligence is a civil law area and to mix civil law with criminal law cannot be satisfactory. The whole idea of what is gross negligence is far too vague with no clear definition being provided in *R v Adomako*. It is still not entirely clear whether the risk must be one of death or merely a risk to health. This offence seems to put far too much responsibility on juries, almost making them 'masters of law' as much as 'masters of the facts'.

> 🖉 This is a reasonable introduction, indicating the different types of manslaughter, but it would have been better to explain what the definition of this offence is. The criticisms of gross negligence are not detailed enough, and the issue of duty of care should have been explained more fully. The final point is stated rather than argued.

The alternative type — unlawful and dangerous act manslaughter — can also be criticised. This offence can be committed by doing any unlawful act, from a minor assault up to causing GBH or wounding under s.20 (Offences against the Person Act 1861). This is far too wide a range of *actus reus*. How can it be fair to have such a broad offence range for such a major crime? A further serious flaw is that the only *mens rea* required is that for the original offence which again could be as minor as recklessness as to assault. The requirement that the act be dangerous is an objective test and also a 'very low-level' test (*R v Church*). Finally, there is no need to prove that the defendant targeted the act against the victim. It is therefore clear that the present law on involuntary manslaughter is not at all satisfactory as both types can be readily criticised.

> 🖉 The section on unlawful act manslaughter, while stronger than that on gross negligence manslaughter, still lacks detailed criticism. The important issue of constructive liability is only hinted at, and much more could have been said about the dangerous requirement, as in the A-grade answer above. The conclusion is weak and some reference to the Law Commission recommendations would have been very useful. This answer would be awarded 13–14 marks.

Unlawful and dangerous act manslaughter

> Now 63 years old, Steve had always been thought odd and unfriendly by his neighbours, Jim and Cath. However, after the death of his wife 2 years ago, Steve's eccentricity increased markedly and his relationship with Jim, Cath and their children deteriorated very badly.
>
> When he discovered one morning that his dog was dead, Steve immediately suspected that it had been poisoned by Jim and Cath. After brooding on this for 2 days, he entered their garden early in the morning and partly severed bolts on their children's swing. During that day, while Jim was pushing his younger son on the swing, the bolts broke, hurling the child and swing on to his sister Helen, who had been watching. Helen suffered a fractured skull and died.
>
> Source: 1995 A-level Law Paper 2 (0625/2), question 1, part (a). Please note that this question is *not* from the live examinations for the current specification.

Discuss Steve's criminal liability for the manslaughter of Helen. (25 marks)

■ ■ ■

A-grade answer

Involuntary manslaughter is defined as unlawful killing without malice aforethought. There are two categories of manslaughter: unlawful and dangerous act manslaughter — also referred to as Church doctrine manslaughter — and gross negligence manslaughter.

On the basis of the facts, Steve would be charged with unlawful and dangerous act manslaughter. The charge cannot be gross negligence manslaughter as this requires a failure to act (an omission).

For a charge of unlawful and dangerous act manslaughter to be brought, the defendant must have committed an unlawful act and this has to be a crime. Unlawfulness in the sense of a tort or a breach of contract would not be sufficient, as confirmed by *R v Franklin*. Where there is no crime committed, there can be no conviction (*R v Lamb* and *R v Scarlett*). In both these cases the defendant's conviction was quashed on appeal, on the grounds that the Crown had failed to prove that the defendant had committed an 'initial' crime which was then the basis of manslaughter.

In this case, Steve's crime was criminal damage. The *actus reus* for this offence is destroying or damaging property that belongs to another. Steve's action (in severing the bolts) constitutes the *actus reus* for criminal damage.

Unlawful and dangerous act manslaughter does not require a separate *mens rea*. There is no need when establishing liability for this form of manslaughter for the Crown to prove *mens rea*, whether intentionally or recklessly as to causing death, serious injury or any injury. The *mens rea* for the initial crime is enough, provided that the crime caused the death.

The *mens rea* for the offence of criminal damage is intention or recklessness. This would now be the *mens rea* for manslaughter. The 2003 case of *R* v *G*, decided by the House of Lords, overruled the case of *R* v *Caldwell* and objective recklessness is no longer part of English law for any offences. It would therefore be for the Crown to prove that Steve realised the risk he was taking when he severed the bolts of the swing.

The defendant's act must also be dangerous in order to secure a manslaughter conviction. This was defined in *R* v *Church* as meaning 'dangerous in the sense that a sober and reasonable person would inevitably recognise that it carried a risk of some harm albeit not serious'. This is an objective test, because it does not take into account the defendant's personal circumstances. Steve's action satisfies this test, as it would have been obvious to a reasonable person that severing the bolts of the children's swing was likely to cause some harm.

Finally, it must be proven that the defendant's act was a cause of the death. Both the factual and legal rules of causation have to be satisfied. Steve's actions satisfy the factual 'but for' test. In addition, his actions were a 'substantive and operating' cause of Helen's death (*R* v *Smith*) and can be regarded as a 'significant contribution' to her death (*R* v *Cheshire*). The legal rules of causation appear to be satisfied, since there is no break in the causal chain which was started by Steve — Jim's son being thrown from the swing on to Helen is a foreseeable consequence.

On the basis of the evidence, it is likely that Steve would be convicted of unlawful dangerous act manslaughter. He had the required *mens rea* for criminal damage and his crime went on to cause the victim's death. The issue of guilt or innocence is, however, entirely up to the jury.

The only defence which on the above facts could be open to Steve is that of insanity, which is defined by the M'Naghten rules. (As he has been charged with manslaughter, the partial defence of diminished responsibility under the Homicide Act 1857 is not available.) These rules require the defendant to prove on the balance of probabilities that, at the time he severed the bolts of the swing, he was suffering from a defect of reason caused by a disease of the mind, and as a result was unable to understand the nature and quality of his acts, or he did not appreciate that what he did was wrong in a criminal, not moral, sense. It may be that psychiatric evidence could support this defence, given that his 'eccentricity increased markedly' after his wife's death. However, unless there was further evidence, it would be open to the prosecution to assert that his eccentricity did not amount to a disease of the mind, in which case his defence would fail. It could also be argued by the Crown that by entering Jim's garden early in the morning, Steve fully realised that what he was doing was in fact wrong, and this would further weaken this line of defence.

A2 Law

question 4

e Note the effective structure of this answer. The offence of involuntary manslaughter is defined correctly, and then the candidate gives full explanations of unlawful and dangerous act manslaughter, making excellent use of leading cases. Each rule is applied clearly to the scenario facts. The candidate explains the defence of insanity fully in terms of each of the M'Naghten rules. The answer would receive 23–25 marks.

Question 5

Murder, provocation and intoxication

> While having a drink in a pub with his wife Nina, Mark was subjected to a lot of rude comments from a very noisy and drunken group of women sitting nearby. Jane was particularly persistent in making sexual suggestions and, eventually, Nina went across to the group and threw a pint of beer over Jane. Mark and Nina then left.
>
> Later that evening, Nina found herself in the toilets of a nightclub at the same time as Jane and called her a 'squint-eyed slut'. (Jane was, in fact, rather sensitive about the appearance of her eyes.) Jane immediately produced a small knife from her bag and stabbed Nina twice. One of the stab wounds pierced Nina's lung and she died a few days later.
>
> Source: 1996 A-level Law Paper 2 (0625/2), question 1, part (a). Please note that this question is *not* from the live examinations for the current specification.

Assess Jane's liability for the murder of Nina. (25 marks)

■ ■ ■

A-grade answer

Murder is defined as unlawful killing with malice aforethought, where the *actus reus* is unlawful killing and the *mens rea* is malice aforethought. This means the intention to kill or commit grievous bodily harm (GBH), which is any serious harm. This extension of *mens rea* to include intent to cause GBH was confirmed by the cases of *R* v *Cunningham* and *R* v *Vickers*.

As murder is a result crime, it is essential for the prosecution to prove that the defendant by his or her voluntary actions brought about or caused the death of the victim. It is immediately clear that the stabbing by Jane was voluntary and so the rules of causation must be considered. There are two rules: factual and legal causation. Factual causation requires the question, 'but for' Jane's stabbing would Nina still be alive? The answer is obviously 'yes'. There are no other factors which have influenced Nina's death. As for legal causation, the present rules were set out in the cases of *R* v *Smith* and *R* v *Cheshire*. These are that the defendant need not be the sole cause of death, but the defendant must be the substantive and operating cause; or, as stated in *Cheshire*, the defendant must have made a significant contribution to the victim's death. In the instant case, Jane has stabbed Nina not once but twice with a knife which was at least large enough for its blade to penetrate a lung. There is no indication in the scenario that there was any medical failure in her treatment, although even if there had been, under the rule in *R v Smith* 'only if the second cause is so overwhelming as to make the original wound merely part of the history can it be said that death does not flow from the wound'.

It is for the judge to direct the jury as to the relevant principles of the law of causation and then to leave the jury to decide, in the light of these principles, whether or not the necessary causal link has been established. In this case, it seems quite clear that Jane's actions meet all the relevant criteria on causation.

Having established the *actus reus* of the crime, *mens rea* must be considered. Murder is defined as a crime of specific intent which requires the prosecution to prove beyond all reasonable doubt that Jane intended to kill or commit GBH. Intention is to be considered under two heads — direct or oblique. Direct intention was defined in *R v Mohan* in dictionary terms as aim, purpose or objective. It is certainly possible that by using a weapon, Jane could come within this definition. However, it is likely that while she may admit intending to hurt Nina, she may deny having the necessary specific intent for murder. This then brings into focus the issue of oblique intent, which was clearly seen in the case of *R v Hancock and Shankland*; this is where the defendant has undoubtedly caused the victim's death but has done so in circumstances where it is possible for him or her to allege that the death was neither desired nor foreseen.

This area of law has given rise to considerable judicial difficulties over recent years as the cases of *DPP v Smith*, *Hyam*, *Moloney* all reveal. The 1993 case of *R v Nedrick* has greatly clarified this type of intent. In this case, Lord Lane CJ stated that the members of the jury are entitled to draw the inference of intention only where they are sure that the defendant foresaw death or serious injury as a virtual certainty. Indeed, he thought that in those circumstances 'the inference may be irresistible'. This ruling on intention was largely confirmed in the 1998 case of *R v Woollin* where Lord Steyn preferred the word 'find' to that of 'infer'. If we apply that dictum to this case, it seems that Jane could have possessed the necessary intent, as stabbing Nina twice and inflicting deep wounds must as a virtual certainty have resulted in death or really serious injury, and this result would have been foreseen by Jane.

Thus it can fairly be concluded that Jane meets both the *actus reus* and *mens rea* tests for murder, but her guilt would be decided as a matter of law by the jury.

As to possible defences that she may plead, there would appear to be two — provocation and intoxication. Provocation, as the more likely, will be explained first. This is a partial defence to murder which is defined by s.3 of the Homicide Act 1957. To all other offences it is only available as a plea in mitigation. If successfully pleaded to murder, it results in conviction of the lesser offence of voluntary manslaughter. The following criteria must be met to prove this defence. First there must be evidence of provocation, 'whether by actions or words spoken'. Here we have the pouring of beer by Nina over Jane's head, and calling her a 'squint-eyed slut'. The provoking conduct must then cause the defendant to lose self-control, which as stated in *R v Duffy* must be 'sudden, temporary and immediate'. This would appear to eliminate the throwing of the beer, which occurred earlier that evening. The fact that Jane immediately produced the knife and stabbed Nina may be evidence of her loss of control, but this question would have to be decided by the jury.

The jurors would also have to decide the second issue of 'the reasonable man' test. This objective test was clarified by the case of *Camplin* v *DPP*, which specifically overruled *R* v *Bedder* and accepted into English law the test established in the New Zealand case of *R* v *McGregor*. According to this test, certain permanent characteristics of the actual defendant are attributed to the 'reasonable person' as likely to 'affect the gravity of the provocation'. Such characteristics are the defendant's age, race and gender, although it is assumed that any permanent disfigurement of the defendant could also be so ascribed, provided that the focus of the provocation was that particular feature, as it was here. This would therefore appear to allow the judge to direct the jury to consider the 'reasonable person with a squint'. This question, as already stated, is one entirely for the jury to resolve.

However, before going on to consider the possible defence of intoxication, the effect Jane's intoxication would have on her plea of provocation must first be analysed. While a drunk person may in law be provoked and thus lose self-control, as in the leading case of *R* v *Newell*, the Court of Appeal made it clear in *Camplin* that voluntary intoxication cannot be an 'attributable characteristic' and was merely a transitory state for which the defendant had been responsible. The effect of Jane's drunkenness would not destroy her plea of provocation but it would certainly have the effect of weakening it.

Finally, as to intoxication itself as a defence, the law does not and never has accepted voluntary intoxication as a defence to criminal liability. The only significant exception is in specific intention offences such as murder, when following from the case of *DPP* v *Beard*, it was held that if a defendant was so drunk as to be unable to form the necessary *mens rea*, then he or she would be acquitted of murder but instead convicted of manslaughter. In Jane's case, there does not appear to be sufficient evidence of severe intoxication on her part to merit such a plea.

> This answer clearly demonstrates the value of a structured approach to this type of problem-solving question. It starts with the definition of murder and then proceeds to consider the issue of causation, describing both factual and legal rules. Case authorities are used effectively to support legal rules. The answer then deals with application of the scenario facts to these legal rules. The issue of intent is dealt with similarly, with explanation of rules and their supporting cases followed by their application to the scenario. The possible defences — intoxication and provocation — are correctly identified and then explained in detail. Note that the candidate includes as much material on defences as there is on offences. In particular, notice the level of detail in which provocation is explained, especially the 'reasonable man' test. Finally, the candidate considers intoxication, first of all within the context of provocation, and then by itself. This answer would receive the full 25 marks.

Murder, diminished responsibility and insanity

While having a drink in a pub with his wife Nina, Mark was subjected to some banter from women at an adjacent table. One of these, Jane, was also behaving very strangely, muttering continuously to herself. Jane had been receiving psychiatric treatment for a severe depressive illness.

Later that evening, Nina found herself in the toilets of a nightclub at the same time as Jane, who suddenly produced a knife from her handbag and stabbed Nina twice, puncturing a lung. Nina died from her injuries 2 days later.

Amendment to scenario in question 5.

Assess Jane's liability for the murder of Nina. (25 marks)

The 'offence' issues of this question are identical to question 5.

■ ■ ■

A-grade answer

Given the fact that Jane was suffering at the time of Nina's killing from a 'serious depressive illness for which she was receiving psychiatric treatment', a defence which she could plead is that of diminished responsibility. This is available as a partial defence to murder and is defined in the Homicide Act 1957, s.2. As with insanity, the burden of proof is on the defence to provide an evidential foundation, but the standard of proof is that of civil law, i.e. the balance of probabilities.

The Homicide Act lays down two separate requirements for this defence. The first is that the defendant was suffering at the time of the killing from an abnormality of mind, 'whether arising from a condition of arrested or retarded development...or any inherent causes or induced by disease or injury'. This is a matter for expert psychiatric evidence and usually two specialist doctors will testify about this issue. In the instant case, the evidence about Jane's depressive illness and her course of treatment would involve such expert testimony. It is required to prove that she was suffering from a condition 'bordering on but not amounting to insanity' (*HM Advocate* v *Braithwaite per L. Cooper*).

The second requirement for this defence is that the abnormality of mind must have 'substantially impaired the defendant's mental responsibility' for the killing. This is a matter for the members of the jury to decide and they may reject unanimous medical evidence that the defendant is suffering from diminished responsibility. This was clearly established in *Walton* v *The Queen* (1978 Privy Council case).

In this case, given the weight of psychiatric evidence, it is likely that the issue of abnormality of mind would be established, but the second test is very much for the jury to determine. If pleaded successfully, Jane would be convicted of voluntary manslaughter and could expect to receive a significantly reduced sentence.

Finally, within the context of her depressive illness, Jane could also plead the defence of insanity under the M'Naghten rules (1843) and argue that she was suffering from a defect of reason arising from a disease of the mind so as not to understand the nature and quality of her actions or that what she did was wrong in a criminal, not moral, sense. Again, this defence would need to be established by expert medical evidence 'on the balance of probabilities' and it would be open to the Crown to seek to refute this with opposing medical evidence. If the members of the jury accepted this defence, they would bring in the 'special verdict' of 'not guilty by reason of insanity'. Under the Criminal Procedure (Insanity and Unfitness to Plead) Act 1991, the trial judge would be required to order that the defendant be detained in a suitable hospital for an indefinite period of time.

> Note how much detail is provided in this answer, particularly on the defence of diminished responsibility. An answer of this quality is rare — answers on defences are often too superficial, almost appearing as an afterthought. Diminished responsibility answers frequently contain little explanatory introduction and most commonly make no reference to the second test — the 'substantial impairment of mental responsibility'. The candidate's discussion of this defence alone would make this answer A-grade standard. The addition of insanity confirms this grade, but you should be aware that under examination conditions you would be well advised to limit your answer to diminished responsibility and then add the defence of insanity if you have time left at the end of the exam. This answer would be awarded the full 25 marks.

Question 7

Malice aforethought

Critically analyse the current law on malice aforethought — the *mens rea* of murder.

(25 marks)

■ ■ ■

A-grade answer

The *mens rea* of murder is defined as intent to kill or to commit grievous bodily harm (GBH) — the former is referred to as express malice, the latter as implied malice.

The first point of criticism is that both these *mens rea* elements are not defined in any statutory form. They are entirely the creation of common law, i.e. legal rules derived from cases. The words 'malice aforethought' themselves are extremely unhelpful, as murder requires neither malice nor any degree of premeditation — indeed, the great majority of murders are actually committed in 'hot' rather than 'cold' blood.

The existence of implied malice (intent to commit GBH) was confirmed by Lord Goddard in *R* v *Vickers* and this has attracted considerable criticism. In the later case of *R* v *Cunningham*, in a dissenting judgment Lord Edmund-Davies argued against intention to commit GBH being part of the murder *mens rea*. He stated: 'I find it passing strange that a person can be convicted of murder if death results from his intentional breaking of another's arm...which would in most cases be unlikely to kill.' He also observed that for the lesser crime of attempted murder, 'nothing less than an intention to kill will suffice'. A further cogent criticism of this issue was provided by Lord Steyn in *R* v *Powell* when he said of this rule that it turned 'murder into a constructive crime resulting in defendants being classified as murderers who are not in truth murderers'.

Constructive liability exists where the *mens rea* of a lesser offence is 'constructed' into the *mens rea* of a more serious offence. This is at odds with the basic principle of criminal liability, the principle of correspondence whereby the fault element (*mens rea*) of a crime should relate to the *actus reus* and the level of punishment that crime may impose — in the case of murder, the mandatory life sentence. It can be further argued that as manslaughter has as its maximum sentence a discretionary life sentence, there is no need for the inclusion of implied malice in murder. The defendant who kills while intending to commit GBH would always be guilty of manslaughter and could, if the crime justified it, receive the same sentence as the murderer.

One further major criticism is the definition of oblique intent. This arises in situations where the defendant has undoubtedly caused the unlawful killing, but has done so in circumstances where he or she argues that the killing was not desired and this result was neither probable nor foreseen, as in *R* v *Hancock and Shankland*. In that case, the defendants argued that their intention was to 'frighten' the strike-breaking miner into striking again, and that they did not foresee that their actions in throwing missiles on to the M4 could result in either GBH or death.

This particular legal problem has resulted in considerable variations in definition over the last 40 or so years, as the different rulings from *DPP* v *Smith* up to *R* v *Woollin* illustrate. The present law is that the members of the jury, if faced with this issue, may 'find' the necessary intent if they are sure that the defendant 'foresaw death or serious injury as virtually certain'. This still cannot, of course, be construed as a definition because, under s.8 of the Criminal Justice Act 1967, the issue of intent is left entirely to the jury to determine by reference to all the evidence, drawing such inferences as appear proper in the circumstances. This means that a jury could decide that a defendant did foresee death or GBH as virtually certain, but could still decide that the defendant did not intend to kill or commit GBH. This position would be unsatisfactory in relation to any offence; for murder, with its unique mandatory life sentence, it is far more objectionable.

> This is clearly a well-planned and fully-explained answer. The candidate starts by immediately addressing the key issue of defining the *mens rea* of murder, stating both express and implied malice. The answer then takes each particular criticism in turn and, by skilful use of relevant case authorities, illustrates and expands on the key critical objections. The candidate's citation of judicial quotations considerably strengthens these points. This answer would receive between 23 and 25 marks.
>
> Take note of the significance of case references in such questions. Without these you are unlikely to be awarded more than a C or D grade.

■ ■ ■

C-grade answer

The current law on malice aforethought is not satisfactory, as there is no statutory definition of intent. The only available reference is that of the Criminal Justice Act 1967, s.8, which effectively leaves this crucial issue in the hands of the jury. The model direction given in the cases of *R* v *Nedrick* and *R* v *Woollin*, which was the defendant's foresight of virtually certain consequences, can be criticised on the grounds that it makes it too difficult for the Crown to obtain a murder conviction. In both these cases, the original murder conviction was quashed on appeal and reduced to involuntary manslaughter.

Another more obvious problem with the term 'malice aforethought' is that it is extremely misleading. 'Malice' in its dictionary sense is not required, nor is it necessary for there to be premeditation. The term simply means intent, either to kill or to commit grievous bodily harm (GBH). This can therefore include the person who kills a close relative in order to spare his or her suffering from a painful terminal illness. The case of *R* v *Cox* clearly illustrates this problem; were it not for the fact that his patient had been cremated, it seems likely that he would have been convicted of murder rather than attempted murder.

A further criticism is directed at the issue of what is called implied malice, which is intent to commit GBH. It has been argued that only those who intend to kill should be liable for murder. However, it has always been the legal rule that those who attack their victims intending to cause GBH should accept the consequences if their victim dies of his or her injuries. By allowing implied malice to form part of the *mens rea* of murder, the law is making murder into a crime of constructive *mens rea*.

> 🖉 The difference between this attempt and the A-grade answer is clear. The first problem is the lack of definition of 'malice aforethought'. The important and central criticism of implied malice is also explained poorly, with no references being made to the leading case authorities. The answer would receive 13 marks.